IMAGES OF ENGLAND

OXFORDSHIRE CINEMAS

IMAGES OF ENGLAND

OXFORDSHIRE CINEMAS

IAN MEYRICK

TEMPUS

Front cover picture: Staff in front of the original frontage of the Electra Palace in Queen Street, Oxford around 1913. The cinema had opened in 1911 and the entrance was widened in 1913. (OCCPA)

Back cover picture: The Palace Cinema, Banbury. The film *Belladonna* dates the picture as around 1934-35. (OCCPA)

Frontispiece: The Regal in Cowley Road, Oxford. This magnificent foyer still exists although some of the features are hidden at present. (CTA)

First published 2007

Tempus Publishing Limited
The Mill, Brimscombe Port,
Stroud, Gloucestershire, GL5 2QG
www.tempus-publishing.com

© Ian Meyrick 2007

ISBN 978 0 7524 4333 1

Typesetting and origination by Tempus Publishing Limited.
Printed in Great Britain.

Contents

Acknowledgements

This book would not have seen the light of day without the enormous and generous help I have received from current and former cinema proprietors and employees, cinema historians and the recollections of cinema-goers of all ages.

Principal sources have been contemporary local newspapers from 1896 onwards, in particular those titles (or their predecessors) that are now published by Newsquest. I would like to express my gratitude to the Cinema Theatre Association archivist Clive Polden and to Rachel Marks for their support and interest throughout this project. Their tireless voluntary work for the CTA maintains an invaluable photographic and press cutting archive of UK cinemas. The Centre for Oxfordshire Studies run by Oxfordshire County Council has been my second home for five years – Dr Malcolm Graham and his staff maintain a collection without which any local or family historian would be lost, and their breadth of knowledge, so willingly shared, has been built up over many years. I hope that those responsible for future planning will continue to realise what an asset we have here, and ensure that it can carry on its work.

I would like to thank (in alphabetical order) the many people have lent photographs, shared memories, provided technical help, searched out answers for me or helped in other ways over the years, including: Marilyn Airstone, the Albany-Ward family, Younis Ali, Sue Austin, The Bartons Local History Group (Chris Edbury), David Beasley, Doug and Vi Beckett, Jeremy Buck, BFI Library, Fred Brooks, Derek Brown, Jim Brown, John and Norma Carpenter, Geoff Chandler, Don Chapman, Chipping Norton Museum (Pauline Watkins), Bob Churchill, City Screen Ltd, Cliff Colborne, Patricia Cook, Michael Cordner, Peter Cox, Terry Creswell, Pat Crutch, Peter Davis, Gill Dean, Peter Delnevo, Elizabeth Drury, Allen Eyles, Leslie Fitchett, Michael French, Jeanne Gibbs, Eric Giles, Richard Giles, Colin and Jean Greenway, Bill Heine, Gordon Hendry, Tim Horton, James Horton, Barbara Imbert, Wayne Ivany, Janet Jeffs, Terry Jones, Julie Kennedy, Sue Kirwan, Saied Marham, Daniel Marshall, Ray Marshall, David Martin, Margaret and Vic Merry, Raymond Moody, Bob Morrison, Gill Moss, Tony Moss, Jessie Newman, Richard Norman, North Oxfordshire Consortium Ltd, Arthur Northover, Oxfordshire Record Office, Mark Pawley, Pearl & Dean, Martin Phillips, Bill Port, H. John Powell, Ron Prew, John Rawlings, John Richards, Tom Ruben, Chris Savory, John Sharp, Suzanne Sheriff, Claire and Matt Shewbridge, Jim Slater, Peter Smith, Vera Storie, Chris Tee, Don Todd, Peter Vaughan, John Warburton, Mike Warner, Kath Wayne, Gene Webb, Michael Weinert, Richard Wilkins, Doris Wilson, Brian Winfield, Graham Wintle, Giles and Rachel Woodforde, Melissa Woodley and to all others who provided information or assistance.

Continuum Books kindly gave permission to quote the extract from *Vera Brittain: England's Hour*.

My grateful thanks are due to Nicola Guy and Claire Forbes of Tempus Publishing for their help, advice and patience.

Finally, but most importantly, to my family Helen, Claire and Emily my love and thanks for their patience and support throughout this whole project.

SELECTED PUBLICATIONS

Two circuit histories are particularly relevant to Oxfordshire:
ABC The First Name in Entertainment, Allen Eyles, (1993, CTA).
Union Cinemas Ritz, Donald Inkster (1999, The Wick).
   Helpful local information is to be found in two booklets:
Early Oxford Picture Palaces, Paul Marriott (1978, published by the author).
The Dream Palaces of Oxfordshire, Sean Currell (1983, Mercia Cinema Society).
   The Kinematograph Year Book (1913-1971) lists operating cinemas and their proprietors year by year, and is referred to as *Kine Year Book* in the text.

PHOTOGRAPHIC CREDITS

These are given with each picture. CTA indicates Cinema Theatre Association archive; OCCPA is the Oxfordshire County Council Photographic Archive; IM is the author. Despite best efforts, it has often been difficult to identify the original source of the older pictures used. Where, inadvertently, copyright holders have not been acknowledged correctly, apologies are extended and they are asked to forward details.

The photograph of the Castle Street, Oxford, Electric Theatre (Minn Coll. Neg 5/19) is reproduced by permission of the Bodleian Library, University of Oxford.

SOCIETIES

Those interested in cinema history may want to consider joining the following societies:
Cinema Theatre Association (www.cinema-theatre.org.uk)
Mercia Cinema Society (www.merciacinema.org.uk)

Introduction

Cinema has been an important part of Oxfordshire life since the first public showing of films in the UK way back in 1896. This book traces that story, from the picture pioneers, through the rise of the big circuits and the super cinemas of the 1930s, the subsequent decline, and up to today's multiplexes.

A number of decisions have had to be made about what to include or exclude; my general rule has been that if a building was open to the public and listed (somewhere!) as a cinema, it appears in the gazetteer. Private cinemas in closed locations such as stately homes, colleges and schools have not been included. Occasional shows in village halls have not been listed although some are mentioned in passing and there is some reference to the travelling cinemas that visited particular venues on a regular basis.

Changing county boundaries have also been an issue – our cinema heritage has been greatly enriched by the addition of the towns from Berkshire through local government reorganisation. If the location is now or has ever been in Oxfordshire, it has been included, although some of the venues covered have never actually operated in the county, a good example being the Abingdon Pavilion, which closed before the war. Caversham was still in Oxfordshire the year its first cinema opened, so is included.

Wherever possible, main opening and closing dates and programmes are given. This proved more difficult than might be expected as many village cinemas did not advertise regularly in the press, if at all; for example, in Burford a film renter's poster outside the hall would suffice to attract the local audience. This was fine at the time, but not so helpful to the cinema historian. In the early days, programme details were not advertised and audiences just came along to see a selection of short films on show, knowing only that it was a 'complete change of programme' from their last visit.

The varying length of the entries for particular cinemas may also come as a surprise. Sometimes, as in the case of the Oxford Majestic, the associated history means that, although relatively short-lived as a cinema, there is a fascinating story to tell. On the other hand, the New Theatre and Playhouse in Oxford have long and honourable theatrical histories but were never mainstream cinemas, so are not dealt with in detail.

An overview of the development of cinema in Oxfordshire is followed by a look at particular aspects such as projection, music and the experience of going to the cinema as both child and adult. A chance to wallow in nostalgia! This is followed by the gazetteer, giving details of the cinemas in each town and village.

I have tried to avoid a dry recitation of dates, facts and figures, although these are of course included and have been carefully checked against contemporary sources wherever possible. Above all, though, cinemas were intended to be fun, so anecdotes and reminiscences of those who operated and went to them have been included. If some of this fun rubs off and readers look at our surviving cinema sites with a new interest, I will have achieved my objective.

Ian Meyrick
Witney, May 2007

One

Cinema in Oxfordshire

THE BEGINNINGS

Two pressures brought us moving pictures and cinemas – scientific and technical innovation on the one hand and the constant desire to present new and novel forms of entertainment on the other. Magic lantern shows had long been popular and became very sophisticated, with the use of dissolving views from one slide to another, changing day scenes into night, winter into summer and so on; mechanical slides using more than one piece of glass moving against another could produce genuine movement, from a beautiful kaleidoscope to comic effects, one of the most famous being a sleeping man into whose open mouth rat after rat jumps and disappears.

Another source of entertainment was Poole's *Myriorama*, a spectacular show using large painted panoramas that were unrolled from one side of the stage to the other, depicting subjects such as travelogues or battle scenes, with the aid of sound effects (including actual small explosions), lighting and music. We know from the Poole family's surviving records that the *Myriorama* visited Wantage (1872), Bicester Corn Exchange – which would eventually become the Crown Cinema (1886) – and Oxford in 1897, 1900 and 1909. We will meet the Pooles again at the Scala in Oxford.

The race was on to produce genuine moving photographs however, and on 20 February 1896 a group of people became the first paying audience for a short programme of animated pictures shown at the Polytechnic in Regent Street, London. The work of two French brothers, Louis and August Lumière, the *Cinematograph* was an instant hit and soon transferred down the road to the Empire music hall in Leicester Square. Other rival shows quickly followed, with Robert Paul's appearing at the Alhambra, also in Leicester Square.

The new medium spread remarkably quickly, using different trade names, but all presenting shows of short films portraying everyday events such as trains arriving and departing from stations, feeding the baby, bathers diving and workers going home from a factory. The important and amazing thing was that they moved as though they were alive, and it is difficult for us now to imagine the impact this must have had on these early audiences.

The first showing of 'animated pictures' in Oxfordshire was on Monday 7 September 1896 at the New Theatre in George Street, as part of a burlesque show called *The Gay Princess*. The advertisement promised 'the photo-electric sensation of the age' and, for once, what we might now call marketing hype was spot on. How many of those who saw those first shows could have predicted that over 100 years later there would be twenty darkened rooms in Oxford alone permanently dedicated to the viewing of this novelty?

Opposite above: The beginning: films come to Oxford as part of a burlesque in 1896.

Opposite below: Drinkwater's New Theatre, venue for the first films in 1896. (OCCPA)

Right: Albany Ward who settled in Oxford at the Empire Theatre in 1900. Note the dual projection equipment: for moving pictures (left) and slides (right). (Albany-Ward family)

Below: 1905: Taylor's *Waroculograph* has moved on from St Giles' Fair in Oxford to Witney Feast. It has been placed next to Ball's American 'Biascope' – an unusual spelling. (Tom Worley Collection, Witney Museum)

The Oxford Picture Palace, Jeune Street, soon after opening in 1911. Still a survivor! (Jeremy's of Oxford)

Moving pictures were at first brought by travelling showmen who toured halls throughout the country. Records show how quickly films came to our country towns – for instance in 1896 at Banbury, in 1897 at Witney and Thame. Animated pictures also became a popular attraction at St Giles' Fair in Oxford before the turn of the century and were featured at Abingdon, Witney and other fairs. They were presented by showmen such as Charles Thurston, 'Professor' Alfred Ball and William Taylor; in 1904 there were no less than six bioscope shows at St Giles' Fair.

An important figure arrived in Oxford at the turn of the century. He was H. Albany Ward, a former assistant of picture pioneer Birt Acres. He had been presenting the film of Queen Victoria's Jubilee for the Velograph Co. throughout the provinces and had decided to find a permanent base. He became the lessee of the East Oxford Constitutional Hall in Cowley Road, changing its name to the Empire Theatre and presenting variety supported by films from the beginning of 1900. This building was later to become the Palace Cinema. Albany Ward (born Hannam Edward Bonner, he became so well known by his showbusiness name that he eventually formally changed it) was a superb entrepreneur, and also ran an entertainments agency and bill-posting company from his Cowley Road theatre. He left Oxford in 1906 to become proprietor of the Palace, Weymouth, the first in the sizeable Albany Ward circuit of cinemas. He later sold out his theatre interests and concentrated on building up a very successful business in advertising. Although only in the county for a few years, he can be credited with running the first permanent venue to show films on a regular basis, and was certainly an important figure in early British cinema history.

CINEMA TAKES ROOT

Albany Ward's successor at the Empire, Frank Stuart, also presented films as part of his variety shows, and in 1910 opened the first hall in Oxford entirely dedicated to the full-time showing

The impressive interior of Kidlington's new Sterling Cinema which was opened in 1938. (OCCPA)

of films, the Electric Theatre in Castle Street. 1911 saw an explosion of new halls dedicated to pictures – the Picture Palace and Electra in Oxford, Witney Electric Palace, the Grand Theatre Banbury and Caversham Electric Theatre. The trend continued with the opening in Oxford of the George Street Cinema and North Oxford Kinema, the Picture Palace Abingdon, the Grand at the Temperance Hall and Corn Exchange in Wallingford, the Cinematograph Theatre Witney and Thame Electric Picture Palace.

The war years slowed down the openings, although Faringdon, Wantage and Banbury gained new picture shows. After the war some of the older and part-time cinemas closed as patrons demanded higher quality surroundings and better technical standards. Bicester got its first real cinema and, as the 1920s progressed, Headington New Cinema, the Grand Thame and the Oxford Super were opened.

THE COMING OF THE SUPERS

1929 saw the coming of sound (in Banbury first!) and with it the building of the 'super' cinemas associated with the 1930s. Prominent amongst these were the Regal and Ritz at Oxford, the Sterling Kidlington and the Regal Henley. Scaled down but well-appointed cinemas opened at Chipping Norton, Didcot, Faringdon, Bicester and Wallingford. War intervened again and, with the exception of the Regal at Banbury which opened during the war years, the cinema-building days in Oxfordshire were over until the coming of the multiplex.

Although some of these cinemas were opened by independents, the large circuits were beginning to dominate the industry. Foremost amongst these in Oxfordshire was Union Cinemas, which had its beginnings in 1928. Under the control of David Bernhard, who had already had a successful career in the wool trade, it built up its circuit by acquiring individual halls and small chains as well as building some major 'supers'. Bernhard followed a policy of gaining control of a particular town by buying all the cinemas and sometimes even building a new one to ward off competition from rivals. Oxford was a case in point, where Union had five cinemas; they also controlled cinemas at Abingdon, Banbury, Bicester and Wallingford. A series of financial and corporate restructurings as well as over-expansion brought the circuit to the edge of disaster and, when David Bernhard died aged seventy-six in September 1937, Scottish solicitor John Maxwell's Associated British Cinemas acquired a holding in the company and took control. By firm management they eventually sorted out the difficulties and the ABC red, white and blue triangle became synonymous with cinema across Oxfordshire for many years. Of the other major circuits of the time, Odeon only operated one cinema (Henley) and Gaumont and Granada were never represented in the county.

DECLINE AND RECOVERY

However, the 1950s and 1960s saw a decline in cinema-going with the advent of television. Both independent and circuit cinemas were struggling, and the resulting lack of investment made many of them less inviting places for an evening out. By 1970 the Electra Oxford, the Palace and Grand at Banbury, the Grand Thame and the Regal Caversham had all gone. The little cinemas at Burford, Charlbury, Middle Barton and Watlington were also lost.

This depressing trend continued into the 1970s, with further closures at Bicester, Caversham, Chipping Norton, Faringdon, Kidlington and Wallingford. It began to look as though cinemas would disappear entirely apart from Oxford itself, but there were some encouraging signs. The old Scala in Oxford and the Essoldo/Classic in Banbury were upgraded and 'twinned' and part-time cinemas opened at Abingdon, Chipping Norton and Wallingford. The 1980s and 1990s saw closures at Abingdon, Henley and Witney but also new part-time operations at Henley and Witney. The Regent at Wantage was twinned and the ABC George Street in Oxford tripled; Henley welcomed a completely new three-screen cinema, a 'replacement' Regal.

COMING SHORTLY...

All good cinema programmes include trailers for forthcoming attractions, and this book is no exception. The twenty-first century has started well. Although we have lost the little two-screen Regent at Wantage, Oxford now has eight screens at its two Odeons (an increase of four) and the Ozone/Vue has brought an additional nine screens. A five-screen Cineworld opened at Didcot in 2007 and similar developments are planned at Bicester (six-screen) and Witney (five-screen).

Some familiar names have gone. The largest group, the former Union/ABC cinemas, have been through a number of company and name changes, being known as Cannon and MGM before reverting to ABC, and finally becoming Odeon.

Although we have fewer venues to choose from, the number of screens in Oxfordshire in 2007 is higher than at any other time in its cinema history. Attendance figures throughout the UK have risen over the past few years and there seems little doubt that the cinema-going habit, which seemed to have been lost forever, is once again part of our culture. The 'photo-electric sensation of the age' which so amazed New Theatre audiences back in 1896 is alive and well.

two

Going to the Pictures

Everyone will have their own favourite memories of going to the cinema, but few will forget the excitement of looking at the 'stills' in their frames on the wall outside before entering the foyer. The need to advertise that the cinema was 'sprayed daily with Jeyes' Fluid for your health and comfort' was long gone, and cinemas had an indefinable but recognisable warm and plush smell.

The tickets were purchased in a spacious foyer and if, as was likely in Oxfordshire, you were in an ABC cinema you had the chance to buy your monthly edition of *ABC Film Review*, containing pictures and news of the stars and forthcoming films, all for a few pence. The programme usually consisted of a 'B' picture followed by *Pathé News* (remember the cockerel crowing?). Then came the ads – the names Pearl & Dean displayed against a brilliant blue sky between white pillars. P&D are still very much in business and have adopted a number of different title styles and backing music over the years. After that came the trailers ('coming to this theatre shortly') – always dramatic, though it was sometimes difficult to relate them to the film that you actually saw the next week.

The intermission gave you the chance to refuel with sweets from the foyer kiosk, or perhaps a Kia-Ora drink and an ice cream by Eldorado, Lyons Maid, Midland Counties or Walls, served by an usherette with a lit-up tray hung around her neck. Then the lights dimmed, the tabs parted, and the big film started. At the end of the evening there would be a short film of the Queen riding side-saddle at the trooping of the colour, to the music of the national anthem; some of the audience stood to attention in their places whilst others scuttled out. Sometimes the 'Queen trailer' was an old one showing the golden coach at the coronation.

SATURDAY MORNING

The Saturday morning show at the local cinema is an abiding memory for many of us over the age of forty; if you were brought up in Oxfordshire, this was likely to have been an ABC Minors Matinee.

In fact, Saturday morning or afternoon shows go back to the earliest days of cinema, when special showings of part of the regular programme were presented. Certainly, Oxfordshire's earliest cinema, the Electric in Oxford, had such shows as far back as 1912 and the Jeune Street Picture Palace followed suit. There was national concern about the suitability of some of the

Above left: A visit to an ABC wasn't complete without your copy of *ABC Film Review*. (IM)

Above right: Pearl & Dean, the name synonymous with screen advertising. The pillars of the 1950s gave way to a series of different styles over the years. (Pearl & Dean)

films at such shows, as well as the effect that cinema-going in general had on schooling and the minds of the young. This led to the setting up of various committees; the transcripts of their proceedings now make rather quaint reading, if only because of the extent to which some committee members were clearly out of touch with the realities of cinema-going.

Children are the adult audiences of the future, so the cinema circuits began to organise Saturday 'clubs' to encourage week-by-week attendance. Union cinemas had a Chums Club and this was superseded by the ABC Minors. Originally, the Minors was highly organised, with allocated seats and appointed block monitors who were responsible for keeping order; they attended weekly meetings with the cinema manager to take tea and discuss important issues regarding the running of the club and choice of films. Cinema managers, in the guise of 'uncle', introduced the sessions and led the Minors in the singing (or, rather, shouting) of the special song; to this day, no veteran of the Minors can hear the strains of 'Blaze Away' without the words coming back:

> We are the boys and girls well known
> As Minors of the A – B – C!
> And every Saturday all line up
> To see the films we like and shout aloud with glee.

We love to laugh and have our sing-song,
Just a happy crowd are we,
We're all pals together,
We're Minors of the A – B – C!
['ABC' was shouted as loudly as possible.]

These very modestly priced shows (only 6d when I went to the Regal Bicester in the early 1960s) were popular all over the country, to the extent that there was a special *Boys' and Girls' Cinema Clubs Annual*. The major circuits all contributed, and the overall supervisor of the ABC Minors, the intriguingly named 'Auntie Andy', writes in the 1948 edition about the choice of programme, 'plenty of action, very little talk, and no lovemaking'.

Regular attendance was encouraged by giving badges and, in the case of ABC, picture cards that built into sets. Special albums were available, and if you presented a completed set to 'uncle' you received a special badge for that too.

Retired chief projectionist Graham Wintle remembers the shows well, watched from the safety of his projection room, first at the Regal and then later at the ABC George Street:

> We were safe enough up in the box away from it all, but the manager had to deal with the problems. If there was a love scene with a kiss, the boys would go wild. The manager would contact us and say 'I'm going to have to stop the show for five minutes while I get them quietened down.'

Graham asked me, 'Were you a Minor? Do you remember the song?' Of course I did!

The independents also ran special shows. At Faringdon, Jim Horton still remembers manager Ted Pawley having to turn up the lights to keep order, so that the picture was all but invisible. With the closure of many local cinemas in the late 1960s, the loss of the Saturday Picture Show was greatly mourned. At Banbury, where the Grand went over to bingo, there was great concern over the loss of the Minors show. Essoldo, no doubt relieved to be in a solo position, immediately advertised that they would be starting a Saturday show. To their eternal credit, this has survived through the various changes of ownership (including a period as Louee the Lion's Club under Classic) and the Odeon still continues the tradition.

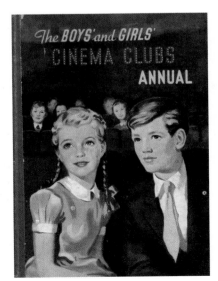

The 1948 annual for cinema club members. Somehow we weren't quite as, well, *nice*, as the children pictured on the idealised covers! (IM)

Saturday morning TV and other rival distractions reduced the importance of the shows by the end of the 1970s. However, independents and the circuits such as Star continued with Saturday shows, and special re-runs of family-type films are still shown throughout the county. But the special atmosphere of the old club – a glamorous highlight in an often drab week – has gone forever.

Above: A selection of ABC Minors' badges. The individual letters were collected week by week and were worn across the chest with pride! (IM)

Left: Cards and badges were a way of ensuring regular attendance at the Saturday morning show. (IM)

BEHIND THE WINDOWS

The stars of screen have always been well served by books and magazines and the work of directors is well documented on the shelves of bookshops and libraries. (Even histories of cinemas are becoming increasingly popular!) Surprisingly little coverage, however, is given to the actual process of getting the picture on the screen, which is after all the whole point of film-making. Ironically, really good presentation is invisible and it is only when things go wrong that most cinema-goers look over their shoulder to the little glass windows. Some of the basic aspects are covered here, partly because it's interesting, but also to help make more sense of some of the references in the gazetteer section.

In the early days films were short and projected on machines that were hand cranked, as were the cameras that had recorded the images. Projectors were later fitted with electric motors to give a consistent speed but there were breaks between reels every ten minutes while the film was changed. As films got longer, a second projector was introduced, enabling the film to be presented without gaps, although some early cinemas such as the Picture Palace in Jeune Street, Oxford, never progressed beyond one machine before they closed because of the more advanced opposition.

Sound came to Oxfordshire in 1929. Two rival systems were available at first – sound-on-disc and sound-on-film. The disc system used large records, playing from the centre outwards, which had to be synchronised with the picture; this was not very satisfactory, as the discs were heavy and breakable. The slightest jog could put the sound out of synchronisation, for which the only effective remedy was to start the reel all over again or abandon the remainder and go to the next one. The rival system, sound-on-film, combined the soundtrack beside the picture on the film and quickly became the standard. The light source for the projected image was a carbon arc, a blinding light created by the arc of electricity crossing the small gap between positive and negative carbon rods.

Architects of the early picture palaces paid little heed to the needs of operators, as projectionists were at first known. The 'operator's box' was just as it sounded, often cramped and very hot and sometimes reached by circuitous routes up ladders and over roofs. The Pavilion at Abingdon was a good (or bad) example of this and I personally remember clambering up the old ladder of the Jeune Street Picture Palace during its closed years and peering into the tiny chamber that used to house the operator and his machine. The term 'the box' is still widely used throughout the trade, even where large comfortable projection suites with rest areas are provided.

Nitrate film was highly inflammable, as anyone who has seen *Cinema Paradiso* will know. After a series of real-life disastrous fires involving loss of life, strict regulations were introduced which included physically isolating the projection room from the main body of the cinema, the provision of fireproof shutters that could be released from any point in the room, and access to fresh air for the projectionist.

Projectionists had a busy life. Each reel of film was rewound by hand, all the time checking for faulty joins, and stored back in a fireproof cabinet. Joins had to be repaired using film cement and would dry out, leading to film breaks, which are rare now because of the use of tape splices. Individual reels lasted for around ten (later twenty) minutes and as one came to an end the arc was struck on the second projector and the projectionist watched carefully for the cues (small dots in the top right-hand corner of the picture). On the first (the motor cue) the second projector would be started so that the two machines were both running. On the second (the changeover cue) the picture and sound were simultaneously switched over. This was imperceptible to the audience and would happen seven or more times per film. But if a reel was put on in the wrong order (or, worse, a reel from a different film!) it was only too obvious.

Above left: The ladder to the projection room at the Ultimate Picture Palace in Jeune Street, 2006. Similar to the original access, it demonstrates the challenges faced by operators at many early picture houses. (IM)

Above right: All mod cons! The original rest room for projectionists at the Oxford Super still exists out on the roof. (IM)

Over the years, technical changes following the coming of sound included the greater use of colour film and the introduction of non-flammable film. The 1950s saw the introduction of the widescreen process Cinemascope (more properly called 'scope' as the former was a trade name of Twentieth Century Fox). This wide picture is produced by 'squeezing' the picture onto standard film using an anamorphic lens, and then unsqueezing it by projecting through a similar lens. Confusingly, the term 'widescreen' was adopted for the process of masking off the top and bottom of the picture to produce a greater width-to-height ratio; this often cut off part of the titles of older films filmed in full-frame 'academy ratio' in the process. Todd-AO, a process using 70mm film and magnetic sound, produced superb quality and is described in the entry for the Ritz at Oxford, the only installation in the county. Cinerama, the biggest of them all, never reached Oxfordshire.

The introduction of cinemas with more than one screen pushed forward the search for automation in changeovers and, later, for long-play mechanisms that avoided separate reels altogether. Two systems are in use, both involving joining all the reels of the film together when it is received from the renter. In the tower system, the joined-up film is fed into the single projector from a large conventional reel. With the cakestand or platter system, the film is placed on a large horizontal 'plate' where it feeds from the centre and, after passing through the projector, is fed back to the centre of a second platter, eliminating the need for rewinding. Carbon arcs have been universally replaced by the Xenon light source for projectors, eliminating the need for changing the carbon rods.

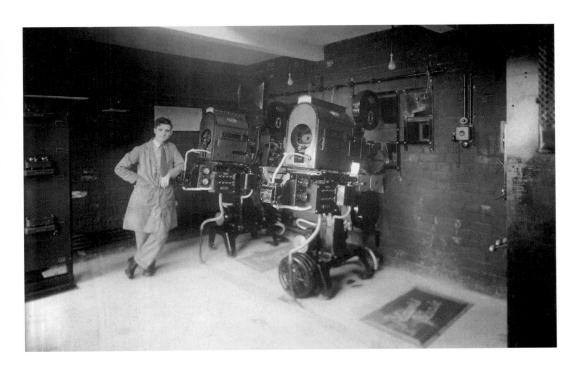

Above: The projection room of the Ritz in Chipping Norton in the 1930s. (OCCPA)

Right: BT-H Supa Mark II projectors with xenon lamps and automatic changeovers at the Scala, Oxford, in 1970. (IM)

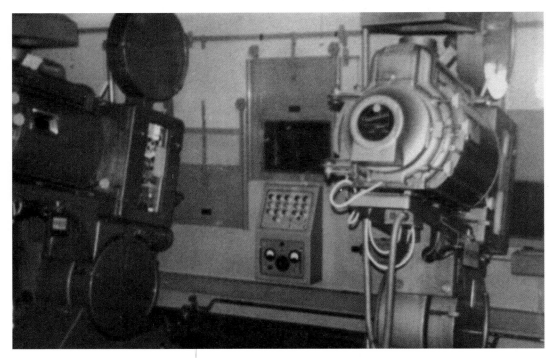

Philips DP70 projectors with Peerless Magnarcs, the 70mm set-up for Todd–AO at the ABC George Street, Oxford, pictured in the 1960s. (Michael Weinert)

Tower system with Westrex projector at the Ultimate Picture Palace, Oxford, 2006. (IM)

Platter or cakestand system with Cinemeccanica Victoria projector at the Vue, Oxford, in 2007. (IM)

More recent developments have included the introduction of the various sound systems, which give superior quality surround sound. Depending on the system, the track is carried on the film or, in the case of DTS, comes on a separate CD for loading on the DTS processor. Sound-on-disc has returned!

The industry is now seeing the gradual introduction of digital projection, which produces very high quality sound and picture, doing away with film altogether. The Phoenix Picturehouse in Oxford was the first in the county to be fitted with digital projectors, in February 2007. It does now seem that physical film will, in the long run, disappear from our cinemas.

MUSIC AT THE CINEMA

Silent films had musical accompaniment (and often sound effects) from the earliest days. The larger cinemas had orchestras, varying in size from a trio up to a full pit of musicians. Some of these names have come down to us through the advertisements and news reports, for instance Archie Payne who directed the Oxford Electra Cinema's orchestra as well as playing solo cello. This group sometimes played in charity concerts on Sundays when cinemas were closed.

Where the cinema was too small to run to an orchestra, we find the pianist. Even though few now remember the silent cinema days at first hand, close your eyes and imagine a silent film and immediately you are thinking in black-and-white, with the sound of a piano tinkling away, fast and exciting for chases and the wistful 'Hearts and Flowers' for a love scene.

Mrs Doris Violet MacDonald was a pianist at Oxford's first cinema, the Electric Theatre in Castle Street and later at the Abingdon Pavilion, playing for four hours at a time without a break;

The way of the future: NEC digital projectors were installed in the Phoenix Picturehouse, Oxford, in February 2007, although film is also still used. (IM)

she recorded her memories when she was eighty-two. Cinema pianists had to have a good ear for picking up and memorising tunes and to be adept at improvising while they watched the picture above their heads:

> When you're playing for a film it keeps changing… you just can't play one piece straight through. You might be playing half a sheet of music and then some horses would come along galloping and you'd have to make up a noise for the horses. You make it up yourself as you go along.

Another instrument strongly associated with cinema is the organ, although there were relatively few in Oxfordshire. Cinema organs were different from their church cousins, having extended ranks of pipes known as 'units', each producing a particular tone colour and selected by the use of different 'stops'. They also had special effects including drums, cymbals and – quite literally – bells and whistles. The console, with its various keyboards (manuals), pedalboard and stop tablets for selecting the various tone colours was on prominent show, and often rose from the depths on a lift as the organist began to play. The emphasis was on the player and console, with the pipes hidden away, whereas a church organ usually has the pipes on display with the organist often out of sight. Although the principles of sound coming from wind pressure and pipes is the same for church and cinema organs, the latter tend to sound different because of the greater use of tremulants that gave the characteristic throb (or wobble) and of a particular tone colour called the tibia.

The first organ fitted in an Oxford cinema had none of the later refinements and was a church-type organ used for accompanying silent films at the Palace in Cowley Road from around 1921. Hubert G. Welch was appointed as organist and pianist in 1926 and recalled in an interview that the organ was built by George Jackson of Oxford. It had two manuals with around six stops on each and, foretaste of things to come, a tremulant. The Palace also ran to a trio of violin, piano and cello, so he was generally providing colour and depth to the performance rather than playing as a soloist.

Right: The console of the Oxford Super Cinema's Spurden Rutt organ was briefly uncovered below the stage by enthusiasts in the 1960s. The stop tabs were still down from the last time it had been played. (Bob Churchill)

Below: The magnificent console of the Henley Regal Compton. (CTA/Tony Moss Collection/John D. Sharp)

The organ was situated to the side of the screen, so he watched the films and inter-titles through a mirror, which could be confusing until he got to know the particular film. He recalled playing for Laurel and Hardy and laughing so much that it was difficult to carry on playing. Newsreels demanded more portentous music, usually a march. At one time, this organ apparently had a glockenspiel attachment fitted to the back of the organ bench.

With the installation of sound in 1930, the Palace management immediately dispensed with the trio, and sold the organ back to Mr Jackson. Hubert Welch believed it was reinstalled in a village church near Woodstock, but searches have not revealed the whereabouts of an organ of this date. However, Jackson undertook work on a number of organs from 1929 onwards, installing additional ranks of pipes, so it is likely that bits of the old Palace organ live on in a number of churches.

The next organ was at the Super in Oxford. This was installed in 1928, soon after the cinema opened. Unusually, this was a two-manual Spurden Rutt 'Organestra'. Rutt was late into the cinema organ market, and this was one of only three installed. The pipes were behind a grill to the right of the screen. After an inaugural concert on Sunday 21 October by organist Stanley Hemery ARCO, films were advertised as being accompanied by organ and full orchestra, and this continued even when sound was introduced, as the supporting programme usually included some silent films. Around 1935 the stage was extended over the orchestra pit and the console was entombed and not 'rediscovered' until a group of enthusiasts uncovered it around 1965, still with its stop tabs down from the last time it was played. It has since been removed and rebuilt and is now at Rounce Farm Barn in Woking, where it can be heard again after so many years of silence.

Organs took on a new role with the coming of the super cinemas where the organ was all part of the experience. The Ritz in Oxford was opened by Union in 1936 and a Compton three-manual six-unit organ was installed, played from a console that rose from the orchestra pit on a lift. It had a Melotone attachment – an electronic device which produced sound by a series of rotating etched discs, giving a rather ethereal sound. There was also a 'phantom piano' on stage that could be played from the organ console. The pipes were in organ chambers above the proscenium.

The Ritz organ was played as part of the programme for many years and was still in use after the cinema went over to Todd-AO in 1959; the resident organist at that point was Albert Brierley, one of a vanishing breed. The Compton survived the fire of 1963 but was damaged. Although ABC initially intended to restore it, in the event it was sold back to the John Compton Organ Co. for spares, the phantom piano being added to a private house organ installation.

Another Compton, installed at the Regal in Cowley, had an even more unfortunate history. Here, the pipes were installed under the stage, and the cinema proved prone to flooding. It was removed to the Ritz, Keighley within the first year of operation, opening there on 28 February 1938. Later on it was moved to Malsis School in Keighley, but the installation was never completed. Unfortunately, storage near a boiler led to the windchests being rendered unusable and the percussion ('traps') unit being badly damaged. The console was adapted to a two-manual church-organ style and offered for sale in 1977/78. The whereabouts of the pipework is unknown.

The Regal at Henley acquired its organ late in life. This three-manual seven-rank Compton came from the Ritz in Tunbridge Wells and was installed in 1972. An illuminated surround and organ lift were added later. It is now in the Burtey Fen Collection in Pinchbeck, Lincolnshire.

Finally, an organ without a cinema. The Guildhall (Abbey Hall) in Abingdon has a Compton organ, installed there in 1966. This was originally in the Gaumont Palace, Birmingham and dates from 1931. A four-manual console and Melotone from the Gaumont, Camden Town in London have been added and a 'vox humana' rank of pipes was later installed from the Majestic at Mitcham.

three

Gazetteer: An A–W of Oxfordshire Cinemas

ABINGDON

Corn Exchange/New Cinema/Grand Theatre

One of the earliest venues for film shows was the Corn Exchange, later to become the Grand Theatre. Built as a general-purpose hall, films were shown as part of a mixed programme of bookings for various events from around 1909. On 1 April 1919, however, it was opened as the New Cinema, with two different programmes weekly, each running for three days. By 1922 the Grand ('where everybody goes') was under the management of W. Annison (proprietor) and resident manager F. Nimsey. The hall had 500 seats and a 45ft-wide stage with a depth of 24ft and 24ft proscenium opening.

Although listed as a cinema in the *Kine Year Book* from 1921 to 1923, variety and concerts were the Grand's main fare, with films being used to fill gaps in the booking schedule or to make up a programme. Charlie Chaplin was obviously popular with audiences, with his films featuring regularly. In 1922 patrons were offered plays, concerts, variety, music and less obvious attractions such as a grand cycling competition. The orchestra of the Electra Cinema, Oxford, visited three times under the direction of Archie Payne (solo cello) to raise funds on behalf of Abingdon Cottage Hospital. The Super Variety show for Christmas week featured Boxing in Barrels ('great fun competition') and two Chaplin films – *Hot Dogs* and *The Pile Driver*. The Corn Exchange survived as a hall until the 1960s when it was demolished for development.

Picture Palace/Picture House/Abingdon Kinema/Pavilion

The Picture Palace opened at 63 Stert Street on Saturday 18 May 1912. The original proprietor was Lew Davis (and, later, the Abingdon Picture Palace Co.); the proceeds of the grand opening were donated to the Cottage Hospital. The opening programme was made up of a series of short films: *Sins of the Father*, *Automatic Removal*, *Caught with the Goods*, *The Broken Vase* and *The Cowboy Pugilist*. The cinema boasted electric light and a cool temperature in the summer. The reported capacity varied between 200 and 300 seats in these early years, with leather covered benches at the front and lift-up seats with red plush at the rear. By 1919 the lessee was W. Thatcher, who undertook a major rebuild, doubling its capacity to 600, and reopening it as the Picture House on 8 July 1920. The cinema was now entered through a 30ft lounge and the auditorium itself was 100ft long and 32ft wide, much of it sloped for better viewing. New tip-up seats had been provided and the white panelling was considered very decorative.

The Corn Exchange, Abingdon, former home of the Grand Cinema. (OCCPA)

The Abingdon Pavilion in the 1930s. Judging by the number of signs, it is not too difficult to guess it was run by Union! (CTA)

Above and below: Abingdon Pavilion in the 1930s. The attractive painted scenes on the walls cheer up an otherwise plain auditorium. (CTA)

At the opening ceremony the mayor, Mr E.W. Langford, speaking to an invited audience, recalled seeing moving pictures for the first time at the Corn Exchange and enthused at how they had improved in quality. The programme opened with a locally filmed scene of the reception given to Abingdon servicemen the previous August bank holiday and 'the scenes, showing familiar faces in the crowd, was most complete and interesting'. The main film was *When it was Dark*, substituted at the last minute for the planned *Belle of New York*.

From September 1921 the name was changed to Abingdon Kinema. In 1936 it was changed, for the last time, to Pavilion and from then on the cinema shared the Regal's telephone number and advertising style, with both being advertised as Union Cinemas from the start of 1937.

A typically basic cinema building of its time, the Pavilion had a floor-tiled entrance and a central pay box open to the pavement with entrance doors each side. A plain foyer included a ladder to the projection box. This was reached by a hazardous route via the foyer roof and through a low (less than 4ft high) door, which opened onto a 3ft drop; the two projectors were on concrete plinths about 2ft high. Former Abingdon projectionist Norman (Gus) Grieve, who worked between this cinema and the Regal, recalled having to 'climb ladders and crawl on your hands'. Projection rooms, even in later cinemas, were often built with a very inconvenient entrance route and inadequate space, almost as though they were an afterthought, even though they were the engine-rooms of the enterprise.

The toilets were through the exit door at the right of the screen, and to reach them patrons had to leave the cinema and cross a coal yard; this also provided an excellent route for sneaking in without paying. Another oddity was a term in the lease by which the adjacent Registrar of Births, Marriages and Deaths had a key to a door into the foyer so that he also could go through the cinema to the toilets!

Photographs taken in 1937 show a long single-floor auditorium with a plain uncurtained screen; some of the lighting was still by gas, controlled from the side of the proscenium. An unusual refinement, however, was the attractive decoration, with murals of mountains, lakes and trees on three walls.

Union's motive for taking on this quaint and outdated hall can only have been its obsession for adding numbers of cinemas regardless of quality and for controlling all the outlets in a town. Certainly ABC was not impressed with this piece of inheritance when they took over operation of Union Cinemas in 1937, and closed it the next year. The last programme, on Saturday 28 May 1938, was *Mr Dodds Takes the Air* and *Wine, Women and Song*. The Pavilion had been advertised under the ABC banner for just two months. The building has been demolished and replaced with offices.

Regal

With the opening of the Regal on 8 June 1935, Abingdon cinema-goers were brought into a different world. The Birmingham architect Harold Seymour Scott and builder T. Elvin & Sons were the team responsible for a large number of small-town Regals, including those at Bicester and Wallingford, although the Abingdon cinema was twice the size of these. All three had been promoted by the same company, of which Mr R. Fort of Bracknell in Berkshire was managing director. Prominently situated in The Square, the well-proportioned wide brick-built frontage was flanked by two shops (Arlington Leather Co. and Marie Viney, a gown shop and milliner) and was impressively lit up at night by neon, which included tulip-shaped motifs. Car parking was provided.

The interior, with seating arranged in three blocks with two gangways, was in stadium style, with a stepped rear section rather than the conventional balcony. Seating was given as 'over 900'. Decorative pillared recesses, rather reminiscent of boxes in a theatre, surmounted side exit doors.

The impressive frontage and stadium design of the Regal Abingdon,
pictured soon after it opened in 1935. (CTA)

Miss Beryl Tombs, the mayor of Abingdon's daughter, in the presence of councillors and other dignitaries, performed the opening ceremony. The opening programme was *One Night of Love*, starring Grace Moore, and *Girl in Danger* featuring Ralph Bellamy.

The Regal was acquired by Union Cinemas in 1936 and passed to ABC the next year. Part-time bingo was introduced in 1969. Full-time bingo had been planned originally, but a variety of protests including a conventional 6,300-signature petition (and less conventional seat-slashing and even damage from a home-made bomb) caused ABC to relent and keep the film side going for four nights each week. Star Holdings of Leeds then ran the cinema/bingo operation until the Regal passed back to EMI Social Centres Ltd from 1975. The writing was on the wall for films with cinema attendances dropping to 400 a week against 1,500 bingo players however, and 28 January saw the last, undistinguished, programme – *Flesh Gordon* and *Torso*. The seating had been reduced from 650 to 236, with tables and a snack bar installed in the lower part of the hall.

In 1977, B&N Regal (Abingdon) Ltd, run by Bill and Norma Carpenter, took over the bingo club. Bill Carpenter had been a director of ABC and latterly headed up EMI's bingo operation; he and his wife Norma leased the Regal on his retirement and ran it until his death in 1981. In 1984 projection equipment was reinstalled and John Carpenter (son of Bill and Norma) and teacher Stuart Jarvis ran the cinema, gradually dropping the bingo side. Later there were a number of openings and closings, but the positively last performance was *Batman*. Even the caped crusader couldn't save the Regal and it closed on 14 September 1989.

The closed and boarded up building, in its prominent position, became an eyesore. Plans by the Co-Op for a supermarket came to nothing in 1992, and in 1998 plans by Paul and Sue Kirwan of the Regent in Wantage to build three cinemas and a Hollywood-style bar and restaurant in the shell, were rejected. Further arguments ensued about developing a multiplex on the outskirts of Abingdon. The Regal had its last publicity in 2002 when children broke into the derelict building, raising fears over exposure to asbestos. This was removed and the cinema was finally demolished in 2003; it has now been replaced by housing, Regal Close.

Astra (RAF Abingdon)
See Services cinemas

The Old Gaol
The Old Gaol Leisure and Arts Centre opened on 29 November 1975 as an ambitious local authority-led redevelopment of a historic building picturesquely situated on the Thames near the town centre. Facilities included a swimming pool, sauna, bar, an exhibition gallery and the 150-seat Little Theatre for drama, music, cinema and meetings. Equipped with 16mm rather than the standard 35mm projection equipment, the first programme was *The Way We Were* (Barbara Streisand) from Friday 12 December. Films were originally shown for three days a week but this was soon reduced to two.

Cinema was never well supported, although EMI had attempted to apportion some of the blame on competition from the Old Gaol when the Regal dropped films in 1976. The manager Michael Henderson denied this, saying that, 'the films shown so far have not been well attended. Our largest audience has been 35' and the cinema had only operated on Regal bingo nights. Despite major structural improvements to the Little Theatre in 1979, the centre's finances were in a desperate state. Film shows were attracting only twelve to fifteen people and were abandoned after the last showing of *Golden Rendevous* on 4 February 1980. Management said that cinema in Abingdon was 'a lost cause' and blamed competition from Oxford cinemas that got the pick of the new films.

The closed Old Gaol, Abingdon, awaits its future in 2006. (IM)

The whole complex is now derelict and boarded up. A plan to redevelop it, including a 190-seat cinema, was judged not feasible because funds were not available. The Vale of White Horse District Council has put the building on the market and had, by March 2007, received over 100 expressions of interest. Meanwhile, the Regal has gone after years of standing empty and the favoured multiplex never materialised. The nearest venues for film have been at Oxford and now, from 2007, Cineworld at Didcot.

AMBROSDEN

See Services cinemas

ARNCOTT (BICESTER)

See Services cinemas

BANBURY

Films came to Banbury as early as 17 December 1896, when the Banbury Old Charitable Society gave an evening's entertainment in the Town Hall, which included, 'Through the kindness of Mr Blinkhorn, an exhibition of the CINEMATOGRAPH or ANIMATED PHOTOGRAPHY'. This show went down very well, and included Cingalese [sic] scrambling and diving for coins, a lifelike representation of boating on the Seine, the procession at the coronation of the Csar and a train arriving and departing. The cinematograph was presented by Mr Joyce of Oxford, assisted by Thomas Blinkhorn, the local photographer, who generously defrayed the costs of the operation. Mr F.T.C. Webb supplied piano accompaniment to the pictures and other musicians completed the evening's entertainment with a short concert.

A delightful rural scene in Banbury Market Place with the Palace Cinema in the centre of the row of buildings, *c.* 1934. (OCCPA)

The interior of the Palace, Banbury, after Union took over in 1934. Note the attractive curved balcony, more in keeping with a theatre than a cinema. (CTA)

Corn Exchange/Exchange Picture House/Picturedrome/Blinkhorn's Picture House/New Palace Theatre/Palace

The Corn Exchange in the Market Place was a general-purpose hall built in the mid-nineteenth century. A local publican, Albert J. Kilby, took it over around 1900 and used it for a variety of entertainments including skating, with films becoming more prominent, leading to a change of name to the Picturedrome Palace of Variety in 1914. Sadly, Albert Kilby was killed at Ypres in 1915; the Picturedrome closed after the last show on 18 May 1916 and reopened on 16 November as Blinkhorn's Picture House with *A Soldier and a Man*, supported by a programme of short subjects and *Pathé Animated Gazette*. This was a real family business, Thomas having been in at the very start of films with his sponsorship of the Town Hall show back in 1896. His son Norman was the manager and daughter-in-law Dorothy ran the box office. Another son, Bernard, helped produce sound effects backstage (once letting a large steel drum used to simulate thunder roll through the screen into the orchestra pit). Tim the dog, another 'family member', specialised in searching for dropped scraps of food after the audience had departed.

The Blinkhorns sold out to The Palace Theatre Co. Ltd, a consortium of local businessmen, in May 1923 and the new company continued with pictures and variety. A further change occurred in February 1930 when G.C.H. Dicker assumed management of the Palace Theatre, introducing British Acoustic sound from 17 February with *The Drake Case*, 'a thrilling 100% "talkie" mystery'. A special children's matinee, the Moss Maachah Trio direct from their great London success, and Rudolph Evans and his orchestra made up a memorable week of entertainment.

In 1934, The Palace Theatre Co. leased the building to Union Cinemas, which continued the policy of films and stage presentations. Contemporary photographs show a steeply stepped, curved balcony; seating capacity was 600 and the proscenium width was 26ft.

Real-life drama occurred on the morning of Friday 6 February 1942, when a cleaner discovered a fire around 8 a.m. The cause was thought to have been a dropped cigarette, which had ignited rubbish in the void between the original flat floor and the cinema's raked floor. Because of the restricted location of the seat of the fire it was very difficult to fight, and the cinema was closed until 16 July when it reopened with the appropriately positive *Smilin' Through*. In later years the sound system changed to RCA, and the capacity was now listed as 794 seats.

By the late 1950s, competition from other attractions was making it increasingly difficult for Banbury to support three cinemas and it was almost inevitable that the oldest would be the first casualty. The Palace closed on 10 June 1961 with *Saturday Night and Sunday Morning* supported by *Brothers in Law*. The main film was brought back by public demand, probably because Warwickshire (just over the border from Banbury) had declined to grant the landmark film a certificate because the producers refused to delete two love scenes. The choice of last film was, of course, a gift to the headline writers – 'Saturday night but no Sunday morning for the Palace'. In the projection room at that last showing was Mr R.H. Kilby, son of the original proprietor Albert Kilby.

After a period of retail use (Palace Arcade) the whole building was demolished in 1979, the frontage being rebuilt in exactly the same style as the original. It is now a bank, and were it not for photographs showing the 'gap' in Market Place after demolition, it would be taken as the original Corn Exchange frontage.

Grand Theatre/Grand

The 500-seat Grand Theatre in Broad Street opened on 18 July 1911 with a mixed programme of films featuring *Zululand*, *Priscilla's April Fool Joke*, topical items including Paris fashions and the Coronation Naval Review at Spithead. The manager was J.P. Lord of Oxford and other directors included J.H. Kent of Folkestone and the mayor of Hythe. Although described as a

The Grand, Banbury, operating under the ABC banner. (CTA)

theatre, it had operated as a picture house from day one. This changed from May 1914 when the management announced that variety turns would be introduced in addition to pictures, a fully equipped stage with dressing rooms having been added. Fully staged shows could now take place, as well as variety turns; for example Billie Taylor's company staged a panto, *Babes in the Wood*, in January 1916 ('Pretty scenery. Pretty dramas. Pretty Girls.' – the publicity said it all). There was also amateur use, when Miss Phyliss Robeson's pupils performed a Matinee Dansante for charity in 1923, her other venue being the Palace Theatre.

In 1929 Mr E.A. Bagley became the proprietor. He was an example of the entrepreneurial independent exhibitor typical of the early cinema and pulled off a considerable coup by the introduction of sound on 21 October with a presentation of *Showboat*. Not only was his the first cinema in Banbury to go over to sound – he was the first in Oxfordshire. Bagley understood publicity and the media; in September 1930 he made an advance public apology in the newspaper to those who would be unable to get in on the next Saturday to see *Gold Diggers of Broadway*, helpfully giving the other dates when seats would be available!

The cinema closed after the last show on 13 June 1935 for 'reconstruction and enlargement as a modern super cinema'. This rebuild was not the result of a fire, as widely recorded elsewhere, and there is no gap in advertising between 1928 and 1935, so it appears that this is confusion with the Palace fire. J.G. Gomersall of Drury and Gomersall, the well-known Manchester architects, designed the new enlarged cinema; it had a balcony and the frontage was designed in an Egyptian manner, one of the exotic styles favoured by this practice for cinema work. The lower pitched roofline of the old cinema is still clearly visible in the rear wall of the present building, demonstrating the scale of the enlargement. The Grand reopened on 12 December 1935 with *Without Regret* and *Two for Tonight* and now had 'nearly 1000 seats' – twice the size of the old building.

The Grand was acquired by the Mayfair Circuit, a small group set up in 1941 after Odeon chief Oscar Deutsch's death, and then passed to ABC on 13 August 1943. ABC continued to run it (including an ABC Minors Saturday morning club) until the lure of bingo profits became too much. The last film came on 14 December 1968 – presumably someone at ABC had a sense of humour to book *Where Were You when the Lights Went Out?* as a final performance, together with *The Biggest Bundle of Them All*. It reopened on 3 January as a bingo hall and over the years was run by ABC, Star, EMI Social Centres and Zetters before forsaking bingo and gaining a new lease of life as the Chicago Rock Café. The frontage has been well maintained and the decorative motifs carefully picked out. The interior is still clearly that of a cinema, with the decorative plaster intact but fronted with rock items. The balcony remains untouched behind partitioning, still stepped but with no seats. The projection suite is intact, including the door to the open balcony high on the front where projectionists could get a breath of fresh air. Although stripped of most of its equipment, the control box for the tabs (stage curtains), the fire shutters and a lone Ross projector base with Peerless carbon arc lamphouse remain as silent reminders of the past.

Regal / Essoldo / Classic / Cannon / ABC / Odeon

The Regal was extremely unusual in that it opened in wartime despite the control of building materials, probably because of the number of service personnel in the area. In October 1940 the Town Council's General Purposes Committee granted a licence under the Cinematograph Act, despite Mr Bagley of the Grand attending the meeting to oppose the application that was presented by Alfred Goodey, the manager of the new cinema. The proprietors were Rickenya Ltd, a very small circuit based at the Arun Theatre in Arundel. The unlikely company name was an amalgam of the first letters of the surnames of the three directors – RIchardson, KENdall and YApp.

Designed by A.P. Starkey and Frederick Adkins, the Regal was built in the historic Horsefair (just over the road from the famous Banbury Cross). Its auditorium was hidden behind a new four-storey block, built in the local yellow stone to blend in with adjacent buildings, the cinema entrance taking up just half of the ground floor width. The Regal opened without a ceremony on 7 October 1940, to the extent that the event was not even mentioned in the local papers! The first programme was *The Four Feathers* with Ralph Richardson and, although initial programmes ran for a week, the local pattern of changing programme midweek was quickly adopted. Seating was for 897.

By 1946 the Regal had passed to S.M. Associated Cinemas Ltd, run by well-known cinema proprietor W. Southan Morris. S.M. in their turn sold out to Essoldo in August 1954, the Regal being included in a £2,000,000 deal that covered sixty-five cinemas. The Regal was, like Rickenya, to be blessed with another laboured amalgamation of names, this time of new owner Sol Sheckman's family – ESther (his wife), SOLoman and DOrothy (his daughter). The Newcastle-based Essoldo group, with its trademark logo with the long double S, grew to be the country's third largest circuit, reaching its peak with 196 cinemas in 1957. The company embraced new technology enthusiastically, being a leader of the introduction of Cinemascope and of projection automation with the Essoldomatic system.

The Grand as the Chicago Rock Café, 2004. It is still basically the same frontage – note the open balcony at the top for the projectionists to get some fresh air. (IM)

The Regal/Essoldo in Horsefair, Banbury, operating as an Odeon 'twin' in 2004. (IM)

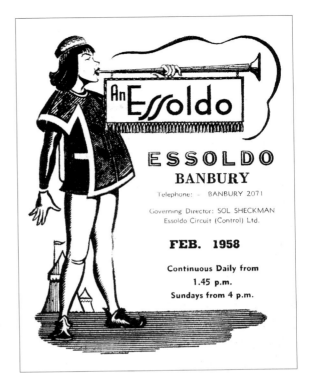

Right: A 1958 programme in the Essoldo house style. (CTA)

Below: Screen 2 at the Classic. This was the old circle extended forward, and originally had periscope projection via a large mirror from a downstairs projection room. This has since been replaced with conventional direct projection. (CTA)

The Regal was renamed Essoldo on 31 May 1956; a further name change came as a result of the sale of the Essoldo group to Classic in 1972 and work on twinning started in the October; on 28 January 1973, Classic 1 (470 seats) opened in the former stalls with *The Godfather*, using the original auditorium and proscenium. Classic 2, being the old circle extended forward, had 241 seats and opened a day later with *Endless Night*. Initially, projection to both screens was from below the circle, with the picture to the new upstairs cinema being via a periscope system up a 'chimney' onto a mirror and thence onto the screen. Such systems – common in the 1970s – were prone to loss of light and definition, and subsequently the original projection room was reopened for direct projection to the new screen upstairs.

The name has changed since – to Cannon (1986), ABC (1996) and to Odeon in October 2001 – but the frontage of the cinema, the only survivor in Banbury, still looks very similar to when it first opened. A big concern when the Grand closed had been the loss of the ABC Minors show. The Essoldo, no doubt relieved at now having a solo position after having also been considering bingo, immediately undertook to provide a Saturday morning show, a tradition that the Odeon, to its great credit, continues successfully to this day. A planned multiplex has never materialised.

BENSON

See Services cinemas

BICESTER

Corn Exchange/Bicester Cinema/Crown Cinema/Crown Hotel Cinema

Like most public halls, the Corn Exchange, housed in the Crown Hotel in Sheep Street, played host to occasional film shows, but was recorded as a cinema venue from 1915. The first press advertisement for Bicester Cinema was for a show on Easter Monday, 14 April 1919 for one night only, featuring a *Victory Drama: Tommy Atkins* and a full programme of all the latest comedies. Prices ranged from 6d to 2s plus government tax (always a sore point). Bicester Cinema (proprietor H. Russell Tomlin) continued to advertise until mid-May, when it was announced that shows would be suspended for the present. The last film was the naval drama *Jack Tar* on 17 May, again for one night only, and the advertised film for the next week (*Verdict of the Heart*) did not materialise.

The closure of the part-time Bicester Cinema enabled the Crown Hotel to pursue grander plans for the building. The Crown Cinema opened on 2 September 1919 to an appreciative audience. The stage end of the hall had been entirely draped with green and gold, and other extensive decorations were in hand. Seating was for 320. All was clearly not entirely ready for this opening night, for as well as incomplete decoration, the proprietors awaited the installation of the new lighting plant by the Bicester Gas Co., to be completed 'in a few days'. A familiar story! The lessee was Arthur Collins, and on the opening night his manager, Charles H. Bowmaker, explained the difficulties he had had to contend with and asked the indulgence of patrons if any difficulties arose while using the temporary plant. No film titles were specified in the advertisement or report, the first title mentioned being a popular one of the time, *Tillie's Punctured Romance*, on 18 September.

Films were shown every night with a matinee on Saturday with prices from 4d to 1s 6d, which compared well with its predecessor. The cinema did well, and the next September issued an

The Crown Cinema in Sheep Street, Bicester. The entrance is through the arch on the right, by the parked car. (OCCPA)

ambitious twenty-four-page souvenir booklet to celebrate the anniversary of the opening. Each copy was numbered, with a lucky number to be drawn at the Saturday night show, the winner to have free admission the next Tuesday and during the evening to receive an unspecified free gift.

The booklet included potted biographies of stars of the day and comments that Charlie Chaplin films had caused roars of laughter to old and young and would be included frequently in future programmes. During the year, over 360 performances had been given, with over 47,500 attending. The writer has a crack at the government, pointing out that £327 17s 11d had been paid over in Entertainment Tax.

Another section deals with the technology of cinematography and calculates that 8,000ft of film was shown at each performance. At this point, the joy of all these statistics goes to the writer's head: patrons are told that 132,000 individual photographs are shown in the average programme, representing 546 miles of film in the year, that 154 miles of film have been hired since opening, and that regular patrons had seen 6,500,000 minute photographs magnified over 24,500 times. No wonder their eyes sometimes hurt!

The Crown (also sometimes advertised in the early 1930s as the Crown Hotel Cinema) continued under a number of proprietors: A. Smith, M.A. Toothill and Alfred Tilt. *The Kine Year Book* entry for 1938 gives uniquely comprehensive specifications for a cinema entry, 'BTH sound, 22ft proscenium, 300 seats, hotel (12 bedrooms), hot and cold, billiard table, RAC and AA appointed'.

By 1942 Mrs M.C. Tilt was the proprietor and she had redecorated and refurnished the cinema. Disaster struck at 2 a.m. on 5 July 1943, however, when she was awakened by unusual noises and found her cinema ablaze. The Bicester fire brigade attended and fought the fire from both ends of the building, running hoses from the swimming baths across the gardens at the back and from hydrants at the front. The wooden roof soon caved in and the brigade did a magnificent job containing the blaze to the four walls and preventing it from spreading to the hotel and surrounding buildings. Another very real risk was that the fire would guide enemy bombers to this highly militarised zone.

All the contents of the auditorium were lost, just the four walls remaining. It was a tribute to the fire brigade that the operating room (so often the source of fires because of the highly flammable nitrate film in use at the time) and the glass roof covering the adjoining hotel yard were virtually untouched.

That was the end of cinema at the Crown, the last weekday programme being *Moontide*, a gloomy romantic melodrama with Joan Gabin and Ida Lupino. The actual last film was the Sunday 'one night' programme which, frustratingly, is missing from its usual spot in the weekly newspaper advertisement. The building was refurbished as a function room and ballroom after the war; it survived until demolition of the whole complex in 1964/65 for a Tesco store. This has in its turn been replaced by Crown Walk, a shopping centre reached, like the old cinema, through an arch from Sheep Street.

The Regal

Popular though the Crown was, the building of the Regal brought modern cinema to Bicester. Like Abingdon and Wallingford, the architect was Harold Seymour Scott and the builders T. Elvin. Mr R. Fort's company was again the original proprietor, but the cinema soon passed to Union and then to ABC.

The auditorium seated 504 on a single floor, with two gangways and a single crossover to divide the front block from the more expensive back stalls. Councillor Morley Smith and his wife opened the Regal at 2 p.m. on Saturday 1 September 1934, the first film being Jack Buchanan in *That's a Good Girl*. The cinema offered continuous performances daily from 5.45 p.m. with separate performances on Saturdays and bank holidays. At prices ranging from 7d to 1s 6d the Regal undercut the ageing Crown, which had to reduce its prices to cope with the competition.

The review of the opening describes the interior as having a warm atmosphere created by the pink covering of the walls, red pile carpet and pink plush tip-up seats. There was generous spacing between all rows and patrons in the best seats enjoyed padded armrests. Also praised were the golden coloured pillars, black and gold dadoes, and the decorative pillars in recesses with reflecting mirrors situated on each side of the screen. There was a sloping imitation lawn in the orchestra pit beneath the screen. Sounding rather like a pre-flight briefing, we are told there are four exits, two on either side in the middle and two by the screen. Certainly in the 1960s it remained a cosy and pleasant cinema to attend, although sadly it later deteriorated through lack of refurbishment.

The cinema owners intended to start as they meant to go on, 'The irritating habit of people talking too loudly to the discomfiture of their neighbours … will be instantly suppressed, and no undue noise will be tolerated by the management'. This resolve was tested during the war, when the Regal proved very popular with service personnel (despite their own Globe Cinema and Garrison Theatre), with queues round the cinema waiting for the previous house to finish. So great was the noise from outside that the audience couldn't hear the soundtrack; a letter to the *Bicester Advertiser* laid the blame on servicemen rather than townspeople.

The Regal Bicester, designed by Harold Seymour Scott, soon after opening in 1934. (CTA)

The attractive single-floor auditorium of the Regal, Bicester. (CTA)

The Regal attempted to deal with the demand by often having three different programmes in a week: Monday/Tuesday, Wednesday/Thursday, Friday/Saturday and a Sunday one-nighter. Extra matinees were introduced at which service personnel in uniform were admitted at a discount.

In July 1969 ABC/EMI transferred a number of their smaller cinemas to Star Holdings of Leeds; EMI took the Regal (now on a mixed cine/bingo basis) back from Star in February 1975 as part of a deal involving 140 bingo halls and passed it to Zetters Enterprises in October 1975. The writing was on the wall; Zetters only continued to run it as a cine/bingo operation for a matter of weeks before applying for change of use to full-time bingo. Managing director David Isaacs said he wished he could keep cinema in Bicester, but the best financial return would come from full-time bingo. '£20,000 will be spent on modernisation, including £5,000 on seating alone. The place is in a terrible state'.

The last children's Saturday show was in March 1974 and the cinema closed on 3 December 1975 with *The Towering Inferno*. After some years on bingo the building closed in 1987 and was demolished in February 1988. It was replaced with flats (Regal Court). Since then, the lack of a cinema in Bicester has, predictably, been keenly felt and a number of initiatives to reintroduce films put forward, including a multiplex.

BRIZE NORTON

See Services cinemas

BURFORD

Burford Cinema

The Falkland Hall in the High Street was built in 1558 by Edmund Sylvester, a wealthy merchant, as his residence; it was later converted into a row of tenements. Burford Recreation Society bought and gutted these, converting the building into a hall with a gallery running round the walls and with a room above. In 1913 the society presented weekly Electric Cinema shows with musical interludes, adding a considerable balance to their accounts. A typical programme is that for 24 February 1914:

Drama: A daughter of the West: Lieut. Daring quells a rebellion.
Comedy including: John Bunny at the Derby.
Entertainment: Two humorous songs by Mr N. Leach.

The town purchased the Falkland Hall as part of the memorial to those who died in the First World War, and ran it as a public hall with a men's institute on the top floor. Travelling shows (Cooke's and later Wickens') visited on Wednesdays.

A permanent cinema was established before the war and local memories indicate it ran until the end of the 1950s or even as late as 1961. There was no advertising except for the renters' posters outside the hall, making it difficult to pin dates down. The proprietor during its prosperous war years was Wilf Barrett, whose day job was at Smith's Industries in Witney, working on the development of an electric clutch. He was also involved with the cinemas at RAF Brize Norton and RAF Little Rissington for a period, and ran the part-time cinema in the Victoria Hall at nearby Bourton-on-the-Water, just over the Gloucestershire border.

The Falkland Hall (centre, with lorry outside), venue for Burford Cinema, in the 1940s. The emergency exit from the balcony is by wooden steps placed against the platform extending from the gable end of the building – not up to today's standards! The projection room door is immediately below. (OCCPA)

Burford residents remember going in the war years, when films were shown on Tuesday, Friday and Saturday. Before the war, seats were not fixed down and there were breaks between reels. Fixed plush seats and a second projector were added during the war years and the cinema was well patronised, especially with 1,000 servicemen being based in Burford. It was a good show with a main feature, newsreel, cartoon and serial. The war itself seemed remote to the teenagers, only really being seen through newsreels.

Brian Winfield and his family were heavily involved in the running of the cinema. His father Bert was a projectionist and his mother Winnie sold tickets. He remembers Wilf Barrett as a 'fixer' who used his electrical skills to keep the two aged Kalee projectors with carbon arcs running. The Falkland Hall had a projection room at the left-hand end (looking from the road) under the balcony, with a door out into Priory Lane. Seating was three lines of hard benches at the front, then fourteen to twenty rows of plush seats. There was a gallery with the most expensive seats above the projection room and down the sides of the hall, giving a side-on view. There was an emergency exit at the back leading to a wooden platform and steps.

Films came via Film Transport, a company based at Witney; they were delivered on Sundays and the programme was 'made up' by Bert. There were two programmes each week after the war, with one print being shared between Burford and Bourton:

First programme: Monday at Bourton, Tuesday and Wednesday at Burford.
Second programme: Thursday Burford, Friday Bourton, Saturday Burford.

Above: The Electric Theatre/Glendale Cinema at Caversham. The new frontage of 1946 is in place. (CTA)

Opposite: The Regal in Caversham; the cinema closed in 1958 after only twenty years of operation. (CTA)

As a child, Brian Winfield was at the cinema most nights; from age fourteen he would operate the projectors. He remembers the film of the coronation coming to Burford. This was a great hit throughout the country as although television had made its mark with a live broadcast, even those who had marvelled at the little black and white pictures were anxious to see the spectacle in colour. As well as public showings, the film was shown to all pupils at Burford School, who came in relays of 199 (the cinema capacity at the time); it took all day. The single print was used for shows at the regular Burford and Bourton venues, plus Great Barrington where Wilf Barrett installed one of his spare Kalee machines, together with Brian, in the village hall. The reels were ferried between the three halls so that everyone could see the film on the same evening.

The Falkland Hall still, of course, stands – certainly the most historic venue in this book – and externally remains much the same, although the emergency exit from the gallery was inadvertently demolished by a passing vehicle some years ago. The lower part was let on lease, without public consultation, for the sale of antiques. This resulted in an outcry and accusations of breach of trust, as the hall was a war memorial and public amenity. However, the trustees needed money for expensive maintenance and had no other source of income so the change went ahead. The ground floor is now a kitchen shop with the gallery blocked from sight by a low ceiling.

CAVERSHAM

The inclusion of Caversham here may come as a surprise. However, it became part of Reading in 1911, having been on the 'Oxfordshire shore' of the Thames. The first Caversham cinema opened in 1911 and on this basis merits a short mention for the sake of completeness.

Caversham Electric Theatre / Glendale

The Electric Theatre at 34 Church Street was opened in 1911 by Caversham Electric Theatre Co. Ltd. Possibly a conversion from an earlier building, it had the typical paybox opening onto the street; external staircases led to the circle and the cinema seated 500. By 1921 the proprietors were Stanley and Brooks and by 1926 C.J. Stanley, who also ran the Empire Cinema in Reading, was listed as sole proprietor; in 1930 he installed sound equipment (able to cope with both the rival contenders – sound-on-disc and sound-on-film). In 1944 ownership passed to Glendale Cinema (Caversham) Ltd under Fred Williams who ran it for the next thirty-three years. Seating was reduced to 300. In 1946 a new frontage was installed with the new name Glendale, proudly moulded on a new external balcony, which ran the width of the frontage, and the sound equipment was changed to the more up-to-date British Acoustic system. The Glendale closed on 4 June 1977 with *Cross of Iron* and was bought by the New Testament Church of God, which retained cinema seating and screen. It is still owned by the church, and in 2006 had a brief return to film for a special showing of *The Passion of the Christ*.

Regal

The Regal, also in Church Street, was designed by architect E. Norman Bailey and opened on 3 October 1938; it had seating for 857 and a 35ft-wide proscenium. The proprietors were Regal Cinema (Caversham) Ltd and it was booked from head office at 141 Bushey Mill Lane in Watford. Controlled by the Mayfair circuit from 1942, it intriguingly gained two additional seats. In 1943 it was taken over by ABC, who ran it until closure on 7 June 1958 after only twenty years of operation; ABC owned four cinemas in the Reading area at the time, and were suffering dwindling audiences. It was initially used as a warehouse; plans to redevelop it as a supermarket, offices and maisonettes were refused in 1971, as were similar later applications, on the grounds of traffic problems. In 1979 Mecca proposed a conversion to a Cinderella Rockefella nightspot, the company saying it would be 'very choosy' about the sort of people allowed in! It was eventually acquired and demolished by Waitrose, who built a supermarket on the site in 1986.

CHARLBURY

There have been a number of buildings used for films in the small town of Charlbury and regular DVD shows are currently operated under the name of ChOC (Charlbury's Own Cinema).

Palladium

The first film venue, The Palladium, remains a mystery. It is mentioned only once, in the *Kine Year Book* for 1927, which would suggest that it was operating in 1926 and closed by the end of 1927. The proprietor and manager was Bernard Robinson and he gave performances on Thursday to Saturday evenings, with a Saturday matinee. Ticket prices were 5d to 1s 10d and programmes were booked at the hall. Researches have failed to reveal the whereabouts (or any record) of the Palladium beyond this one mention, which means that it may have been a rather pretentious name for a venture which was set up in a barn or pub meeting room and did not survive for long.

Victory Hall

The Victory Hall was the cinema that never was. A small hall opposite the Royal Oak in Church Street, it was used for dances and other social occasions but had been built with a proper projection room. There were plans to open it as a public cinema, but to get a cinematograph licence it required an emergency exit, which would have had to go through the garden of neighbour Frank Bailey, who declined. However, a theatre licence was granted for six months from 30 June 1933. Some shows, using 16mm film, were given by the vicar (the Revd Thomas Wood) during the war, with the church projector operated by Vic Merry as projectionist. Soldiers were billeted there and the army laid on dances as well as children's parties at Christmas. The building eventually fell into decay and was demolished; a house now stands on the site.

Town Hall Cinema

The Town Hall was never, as its name would suggest, a municipal building. It was a corrugated iron meeting and lecture room built by the Quakers and situated behind the former Royal Oak pub in Church Street, which they had converted to the Royal Oak Coffee Tavern; it was also listed in Kelly's Directory as the Temperance Hotel. Francis (Frank) Powell Jeffs and his wife May took over as caretakers of the hall and lived in the Royal Oak from around 1938; they founded and ran the Town Hall Cinema from 1939 until 1960.

Above: The Royal Oak in Charlbury, home to the Town Hall Cinema, which was entered from a lane round the corner. Decorated for the coronation, the cinema is showing the 1938 Hitchcock classic *The Lady Vanishes.* (Janet Jeffs)

Right: A Town Hall Cinema poster from the 1950s. (Giles Woodforde)

TOWN HALL CINEMA

Proprietor : F. P. JEFFS   **CHARLBURY**   Phone : 280

❋ **Wide Screen Presentation** ❋

Mon. & Tues. Mar. 30. & 31.   At 7-30 p.m.

Dirk Bogarde, Dorothy Tutin
(U)

A TALE OF
TWO CITIES

Period Melodrama with Cecil Parker, Stephen Murray, Paul Guers

William Sylvester, Richard Leech
Marla Landi
in   (U)

Dublin Nightmare

Crime Melodrama

Thurs. April 2. for 3 days.   At 7-30 p.m.

Frankie Vaughan, Jean Dawnay
in   (U)

Wonderful Things

Romantic musical with Jeremy Spenser, Jackie Lane

Huntz Hall & the Bowery Boys
in   (U)

FIGHTING TROUBLE

Comedy

Prices of Admission : 2/6, 2/1 & 1/3
CHILDREN UNDER 14, WITH PARENTS 1/3
2/6 & 2/1 Seats may be Reserved

Preece & Sons, Printers, Milton · under · Wychwood,

The Town Hall was built at the bottom of the Royal Oak garden and was reached through a small yard just round the corner in Park Street. Vic Merry, who worked as a projectionist before being called up, remembers the building and projection equipment well. Frank Jeffs had built a lean-to projection room behind the stage and 'turned the hall round' so that the stage now became the back of the auditorium, providing a raised viewing area for the best seats. Two Kalee projectors with carbon arcs and RCA sound were installed. The walls were rebuilt with concrete blocks, but the roof remained corrugated iron, a feature remembered by Charlbury cinemagoers because the soundtrack became difficult to hear in heavy rain. Originally furnished with moveable seats, Mr Jeffs later introduced raked flooring and brought in proper plush tip-up seats, some of which were collected from a bombed-out London cinema.

Because of its name, the army requisitioned the Town Hall and garden as an army catering HQ, but after an appeal from Mr Jeffs that they were taking away his livelihood it was returned to him for cinema use; the army continued to present ENSA concerts, a stage being erected and removed for these events. The Royal Oak was also the local ARP headquarters because it had a telephone, and a sheet of cinema headed notepaper still exists listing the special codes denoting various instructions to signal invasion by ringing the church bells, to destroy petrol pumps etc.

The Town Hall showed two programmes each week – Monday/Tuesday and Thursday to Saturday, with a Saturday matinee. There were no shows on Wednesday or Sunday. The full-value programme consisted of a main feature, B-feature, *Gaumont-British News* and trailers. There were 210 seats on the one floor, including the raised former stage area at the back, and a 10ft-wide glass beaded screen. Seats could be reserved (a piece of paper was pinned to the back of the seat) and the back two rows were exclusively used by courting couples. The cinema never went over to cinemascope, although it did introduce widescreen in common with other cinemas. Janet Jeffs recalls, 'One man's constant plea was "Roll on the As! Roll on the Xs!" but my father never, to my knowledge, booked X-certificate films because of the composition of the Charlbury audiences – and probably mostly because my mother wouldn't let him do so.'

Frank and May Jeffs also sold sweets, cigarettes and ice creams from their shop in the Royal Oak and, being a skilled radio engineer, he provided public address systems for local fêtes and gymkhanas. On one occasion, he was using the cinema amplifier, which he had built himself, and had two punctures on the way back. The show started with the trailers being run without sound, the amplifier arriving just in time for the feature. At one time the Jeffs made their own ice cream, and the smell of hot chocolate for the choc-ices has remained with Janet Jeffs. Later they sold Lyons Maid, bought in large blocks and carved up before being put between two wafers (a popular way of serving ice cream, known as a wafer or sandwich). Margaret Merry remembers that, 'you ordered your ice cream when you bought your ticket from Mrs Jeffs, and it would be delivered to you in the interval – if you were in the middle of a row it would be passed along from hand to hand, wrapped in a piece of grease-proof paper'.

In October 1942, audiences for a week totalled 562 people; for the equivalent week in 1956 this had dropped to 503. As the 1950s progressed, the long queues dwindled to the extent that audiences were sometimes as low as three or four on a Tuesday night. Inevitably, the Town Hall became unviable and showed its last programme in December 1960. The house remains as Royal Oak Cottage, but the cinema was demolished and the site is now garden. However, even after nearly fifty years, many older Charlbury residents remember both the little cinema and Frank Jeffs, who had worked so hard to entertain them, with great affection.

CHILDREY

Gaiety

Early film shows and dances were held at George's Hall (owned by George Rowland and nicknamed 'St' George's Hall). Later, around 1929, a large 'tin hut' in a field at Stowell (now known as Stow Hill) was fitted up for films and became known as the Gaiety; this name seems to have started as a joke but it stuck, and the Gaiety Cinema Childrey is listed in the *Kine Year Book* for 1930 and 1931 under Wantage. No further details are given beyond the bare entry, but Jeanne Gibbs, lifelong Childrey resident and collector of local history of the village, remembers that her aunt, Olivia Margaret Booker, used to play piano accompaniment for silent films. The building remained standing for many years after it closed as a cinema and naturally was a magnet for youngsters, who were told off for playing in it. Both George's Hall and the Gaiety have long disappeared.

CHIPPING NORTON

Picture House

Chipping Norton's first cinema was the Picture House in London Road, which was opened on a part-time basis in the Oddfellows' Hall, a general-purpose hall with a simple stage that had been opened around 1910. A photograph of the staff dated 'circa 1912' indicates that the cinema was operating very early in the hall's existence on a part-time basis under the management of Mr and Mrs George Travers. The flat-floored hall, without balcony, was fitted out with 300 seats, a sloping floor being installed at some later point. The Picture House was taking newspaper advertising for shows (Thursday to Saturday only) from 12 February 1919 onwards and around 1921 was acquired by James Grant, in association with Mr T. Strickle. James Grant's son, T. W. Grant, acted as manager and had taken over from his father as proprietor by 1929. He fitted British Acoustic sound in 1930 and continued running the cinema until May 1948 when he sold out to Kinetours Ltd, which already owned the opposition, the nearby and more modern Ritz.

They initially stopped Sunday showings at the Picture House and the two cinemas took one block advertisement giving the telephone number of the Ritz for both. Clearly, the Picture House was the poor relation, although Kinetours did invest by replacing the BA sound system with Mills in 1949. The Picture House reverted to separate advertising in 1949 (but still with the Ritz's telephone number) and soldiered on until a final one-day booking of *The Falcon's Alibi* and *Genius at Work* on Sunday 28 May 1950. On 12 October of the same year, it reopened as the Norton Hall for dancing, the Gala Opening Night featuring the music of Stan Rogers and the Blue Star Orchestra. Tickets were available from the Ritz Cinema. The Oddfellows' Hall survives as offices; it remains a handsome building which has never looked like a cinema.

New/Ritz/Regent

The New Cinema, built on the site of gardens and a tennis court, opened in New Street in the town centre on 3 December 1934 and was officially opened by the mayor and mayoress, Councillor and Mrs Albert Swann. The architects were Seth & Spooner and the first attraction was Eddie Cantor in the musical farce *Roman Scandals*. Set in gardens with rockeries that sloped away from the road, the New was unusual in that the foyer was reached via a bridge from the road. The 506 seats were arranged on one floor, but with the best seats on a stepped stadium design at the rear. The Ritz (later Regent) Café was over the road on the corner of New Street; this opened in January 1949 and was considered a great innovation, the local paper praising the wonders of its automatic toaster!

The Oddfellows' Hall, Chipping Norton, 2000. It hasn't really changed in outward appearance from the earliest days; the large windows were there even when it was the Picture House. (IM)

The caption on this photograph introduces 'Mr and Mrs George Travers, centre, with staff, circa 1912'. They don't quite seem to have got the knack of looking at the camera! (Chipping Norton Museum)

A rare picture of the interior of the Picture House, *c.* 1920. Photographer Frank Packer caught the moment with his flashlight. (Chipping Norton Museum)

New Cinema (Chipping Norton) Ltd handed over to Cecil H. and M.E. Elgar in 1945, who changed the British Talking Pictures sound system to British Acoustic. In a further change the next year Kinetours of 145 Wardour Street, London took over; they renamed the New Cinema the Ritz and operated it for some years, also acquiring the Picture House and running the two in tandem. The managing director was Mr E.R. Mills. Kinetours sold the cinema in July 1953 to the Wantage-based Regent circuit run by Aubrey (Jock) Beardsley and Ralph Austin. The latter moved from Wantage and settled in Chipping Norton, running the cinema for the rest of its life. The name was changed to Regent in September 1953 and twenty years later it showed its last programme on 22 September 1973 – *When Eight Bells Toll* and *Puppet on a Chain*. According to newspaper reports the site, together with the café (which was run by Mrs Austin), was sold as part of a £250,000 property deal.

After a period as The Regent Squash Club, the building was demolished and developed for housing, the old cinema commemorated by the name Regent Court.

The Theatre

The Theatre in Spring Street started life as a Salvation Army Citadel, built in 1888 and closed by the Salvationists in 1962. After a period as a furniture warehouse it fell derelict until discovered by actors John and Tamara Malcolm who set up a trust to develop live theatre in this small community, supported by film shows. Their vision turned to reality when The Theatre was officially opened on 29 August 1979. It seated 118 in the balcony and ninety-eight in the stalls. Early films were projected using a 16mm long-play projector, opening with *The Towering Inferno*. However, the projected picture lacked the clarity and brightness of full-size 35mm and a pair of second-hand GB Kalee 37 projectors, with changeovers, brought film shows up to a suitable standard.

The New Cinema, Chipping Norton, in its Regent days under Ralph Austin and Jock Beardsley. The film is *The Poseidon Adventure* so the picture dates from the 1970s. (OCCPA)

The New/Ritz/Regent had a stadium type design on a single floor. The photograph dates from the 1940s. (OCCPA)

The Theatre, Chipping Norton. Its former life as a Salvation Army citadel is very clear. (IM)

A £678,520 lottery grant and other fundraising enabled major works to be undertaken in 1996 and these included improved stage facilities with a flown screen at the front of the stage. Projection is now by a Cinemeccanica machine with tower system, eliminating the need for reel changeovers. The auditorium seats ninety-eight in the gallery and 134 in the stalls.

These bare facts do not do justice to the atmosphere of this little theatre, with its murals of audiences in their boxes by Graham Rust and other attractive décor. Nor do they pay tribute to the vision and achievement of successfully bringing live theatre and cinema to a small town like Chipping Norton since 1979, and no doubt for many more years to come.

DIDCOT

Coronet

Cinema was brought to Didcot by the Cullen family, who had realised that this new form of entertainment was becoming very popular and lucrative. Henry Cullen, a builder, had been responsible for clearing the closed Picture Palace in Jeune Street, Oxford, and apparently brought the old abandoned projector home for interest. His brother William E. Cullen proceeded to buy over six acres of orchard in what is now the town centre, and his son Hector – who owned a gentlemen's outfitters in the Broadway – sold his shop to raise the capital to build a cinema on the site.

W.E. Cullen & Sons opened the Coronet on Monday 25 October 1926 with *Half-Way Girl* starring Doris Kenyon and Lloyd Hughes. It was a great success from day one.

CORONET CINEMA
DIDCOT.

Manager - - ERNEST W. JEFFS

Continuous
Performance
Nightly
from 6 p.m.

Admission :
6d. & 9d.
(no half-price)
1/3, 1/6,
(Children 9d.).
1/10
(Children 1/3)

Matinee
Saturday
at 2.30.
Children
3d. & 6d.

Covered
Accommo-
dation for
Cars and
Cycles

PROGRAMME

For the Month of NOVEMBER 1927. With Compliments of the Management

A programme from the original Coronet in Didcot. (Norma and John Carpenter)

A report of the opening week sums up:

> The building is a very handsome one, and has seating accommodation for 500. Covered accommodation was provided for cars and cycles. On the opening night, every available seat was taken, and the attendance has been well maintained. A long-felt want has thus been supplied, and it is hoped that this venture will meet with every success.

By later standards, the Coronet looked rather quaint, with its village-hall appearance relieved by a small pillared entrance portico with open balcony above. The cinema prospered, with sound being introduced on 20 October 1930 with the film *Three Live Ghosts*. By this point, the Cullens had realised the full potential for cinema in Didcot and set about planning a much bigger and better cinema on their land, literally next door. The Coronet closed on 17 December 1933 with a one-day Sunday programme, *The Crooked Circle* and *Excess Baggage*. The latter was described as 'a murder that wasn't, a trunk, and a crazy detective in a mix up of mirth'. Seating capacity had dropped from the opening figure (perhaps exaggerated) of 500 to 400 by the time the cinema closed.

This was not the end of the line for the building, which became the Coronet Ballroom for many years, after which it was a Co-Op store before being demolished to make way for the new Didcot Library, which opened in 1992.

New Coronet

The replacement Coronet (imaginatively called the New Coronet) opened nine days later on 26 December 1933. The double bill was the comedy *Out all Night* and a Tom Mix drama, *Hidden Gold*. This opening was not without its own drama. Hector Cullen was refused an operating licence on 22 December and a special court sat on Saturday 23 December following a rush to complete alterations to meet the regulations. A wooden ladder had now been provided as a safety

The New Coronet stands beside its predecessor on the left. The Broadway is still fairly rural at this stage. (IM)

exit from the balcony, Hector having given an undertaking to replace it with an iron one. This is rather a puzzle, as the present building has exits from the balcony and projection room on both sides which appear to be part of the original structure. Possibly the work on one of the staircases was not complete and the ladder was only a stopgap measure.

The New Coronet was designed by Oxford and Abingdon architect A. Buller West. Seating was for 750 (150 in the balcony and 600 in the stalls). The front was rendered in coloured cement finish with a green opaline glass surround to the entrance, which had a light canopy over it, no longer in place. The joinery work was finished with tinted and polished oak, and the auditorium had a stepped ceiling in celotex sheets for acoustic purposes. Three programmes were presented weekly, Sunday, Monday–Wednesday and Thursday–Saturday, with matinees on Wednesday and Saturday.

In April 1936 the Cullens sold to Shipman & King, a London-based circuit specialising in cinemas in country towns, although Hector continued as manager. Shipman & King operated the cinema successfully until 1974 when, by now part of EMI, they announced its closure with no plans for the building's future. An application for a bingo licence in 1971 had been granted (but not taken up) despite stiff opposition from patrons. The cinema closed on 2 March 1974, with a protest 'funeral service' being held on the steps after the final matinee, *Holiday on the Buses*, a lack-lustre spin-off from a television sit-com. A 1,287-signature petition was handed to manager/projectionist George Hurry, who had worked at the New Coronet for twenty-two years.

Although Shipman & King appeared unmoved by the petition, they had in fact entered into negotiations with two Northampton businessmen, Sidney and Myer Cippin (pronounced 'sippin'), who had long experience in the entertainment industry. They planned to develop it as a community leisure centre, reopening for films on 28 October 1974 with *Herbie Rides Again* and *Run, Cougar, Run*. Part-time bingo and occasional wrestling were also introduced.

Myer, who used to come over to Didcot regularly from his base in Northampton, collapsed and died on his way home on 11 April 1977. His surviving brother Sidney continued the business

The New Coronet, on bingo for many years, is beautifully maintained by the Carpenter family. (IM)

Although fitted out as a bingo and social club, the New Coronet (pictured here in 2006) still maintains its original cinema feel. (IM)

for a while, but in 1980 the cinema was taken over by Harwell-based B&N Regal (Abingdon) Ltd who already ran a bingo hall. The Carpenter family have run the operation since then, at first presenting both films and bingo, but eventually settling down to bingo only. In 1985 they resisted an approach by Oracle Leisure to use the building as a snooker and pool club, stating that up to 1,000 people played bingo each week, with around 200 coming to films.

The New Coronet is beautifully maintained inside and out, in marked contrast to many older cinema buildings. Its external appearance remains much the same as when it opened back in 1933 and the auditorium, although fitted with tables and a snack bar, retains its cinema atmosphere. Up in the projection room, the complete set-up of a 1950s-style box with two Kalee Model 12 projectors and Peerless carbon arcs remains as a time capsule of the technology of fifty years ago. Hector Cullen himself died in 2000 at the ripe old age of ninety-nine.

Cineworld

A five-screen cinema on Station Road was included as part of the major new town centre redevelopment which includes the Orchard shopping centre. South Oxfordshire District Council invested £5 million in building the cinema, which opened with a private showing to invited guests on 1 May 2007. All auditoria are located at ground-floor level, with a first-floor central projection suite equipped with Strong Century projectors and platters. There is also digital projection to one screen. Seating capacity on opening was Screen 1: 219, 2: 179, 3: 137, 4: 93 and 5: 270. Doors opened to the public on 4 May, the first programme including *Spiderman 3*, *The Painted Veil* and *Mr Bean's Holiday*.

FARINGDON

The Cinema/Faringdon Electric Cinema/Faringdon Corn Exchange Cinema

The Corn Exchange was opened in December 1863 on the site of an old coaching inn, the Green Dragon. In 1914 the hall was rented for use as a cinema, opening on 13 April (Easter Monday) with 350 seats to a full house with *In the Midst of the Jungle*. Although there were films most nights, charity concerts and dances also took place, particularly during the war years. On 5 April 1915 the live entertainment included a vocalist, eccentric comedian and Little Gladys, clogdancer and cornettist – a feast indeed!

Early proprietors included a Mr Barnard and then the Pollard family, trading as Faringdon Rural Entertainments Ltd. Mrs Pollard took the money, with Mr Pollard playing the piano to accompany the silent films; their son later took over the running of the cinema. By 1923 the proprietor and resident manager was Percival J. Carter, who later went on to set up a small circuit based in Dorset, running a number of cinemas including Shaftesbury, Sherbourne, Gillingham and Blandford.

He was followed by Oram Bailey and, finally, Merle Elliott. Elliott must have been pleased with the business at the Corn Exchange, for in 1935 he closed the cinema and opened the purpose-built Rialto in Gloucester Street, just over the road. The last film was Cary Grant in *Wings in the Dark* on 18 September 1935. *One Hour with You*, the Maurice Chevalier film booked for the second half of the week, was postponed, to be shown at the Rialto at a later date. Seating capacity on closing was 300.

The Corn Exchange was a single-level, flat-floored hall. Projection was from the auctioneer's gallery, with raised seats either side remembered fondly as 'the cosy (or cuddly) corner', popular with courting couples. Sacks used for the storage of grain were also stacked there, attracting rats, which occasionally livened up the back-seat action!

Left: The New Coronet projection room remains intact, complete with Kalee projectors with Peerless arcs. (IM)

Below: The five-screen Cineworld, Didcot, nearing completion in February 2007 in readiness for the opening in May. (IM)

The Cinema in the Corn Exchange at Faringdon, *c.* 1925. The building still stands but there is no sign of its cinema past inside. (Jim Brown Collection)

The frontage of the Corn Exchange remains unchanged and it is still used as a public hall. It was bought by the parish council for a bargain £1,000 when the Faringdon Corn Exchange Co. went into voluntary liquidation the year after the cinema closed. The interior shows no trace of its former cinema use, and both the auctioneer's gallery and cuddly corner are no more.

Rialto/Regent

Merle Elliott's new Rialto Cinema was in a different class, both in terms of comfort and physical structure. It was a steel frame building with wire-cut fletton (brick) cladding and an asbestos tile roof on steel trusses, from which was hung a suspended ceiling of insulation board. It was a very efficient space-enclosing structure and, in contrast to the old cinema, probably the most modern building to be erected in the town between 1938 and 1960. The frontage was painted white and the key to the interior decorative scheme was simplicity, using pearl grey and gold, relieved by white panels; the seats and screen tabs (curtains) were in shades to match.

The opening report gives the seating as 325, although this varied in trade journals from 356 to 450. With all the seats on a single floor, the lower figures are the most likely. The opening was a star-studded occasion. Lord Berners of Faringdon House performed the opening ceremony in conjunction with actor Stewart Rome, who lived in Newbury. Rome appeared in 122 films in a career spanning 1914 to 1950, although he was not in the opening attraction, *The Lives of a Bengal Lancer*, which starred Gary Cooper. Berners brought a house party to the opening, which included poet John Betjeman (who recorded the event in a letter to his wife), the Duchess of Westminster and Adele Astaire, sister of Fred.

The Rialto/Regent, Faringdon awaits demolition. Films have long gone and now bingo has departed. (Terry Creswell)

Lord Berners said:

> For several years now I have been a regular patron of the old cinema in the Corn Exchange, and much as we have appreciated the quaint and somewhat ecclesiastical atmosphere, there is no doubt that we now have a hall worthy of the noble town of Faringdon.

The crowd that turned out for the opening was the largest seen in Faringdon and the police had difficulty keeping them under control. Hundreds were turned away and the crush was so great that Mrs Horton, a staff member who had transferred over from the Corn Exchange, fainted and was carried out over the heads of the crowd.

Aubrey Beardsley of Wantage had added the Rialto to his circuit by 1948, changing the name to Regent. His manager was Edward (Ted) Pawley, who came from the film industry where he had been a sound recording engineer. His name is still regularly seen in credits as he recorded the innovative soundtrack for the classic John Grierson film *Night Mail*, with music by Britten and poetry by Auden.

Mark Pawley recalls:

> Each member of the family worked there in some role or other. My brother and I became projectionists [Kalee 8 projectors with carbon arcs] whilst my two sisters were usherettes. My mother and father took turns in the kiosk and the ticket office.

Ted Pawley was fastidious about the cleanliness of the forecourt and, when a car parked under the no-parking sign, was known on occasion to stick a potato up the exhaust. When the owner

The VIP seats at the Rialto, Faringdon on the opening night, 18 September 1935.
Back row, from left to right: Lady Birkenhead, Vivian Jackson, Lady Mary Lygon, John Betjeman,
Loelia Duchess of Westminster, Robert Heber-Percy. Front row: Lady Dorothy Lygon, Adele
Astaire, Lord Berners, Stewart Rome. (Jim Brown Collection)

The interior of the Regent, Faringdon, c. 1953. Note the smart festoon curtain in the raised position.
(Mark Pawley)

returned, there would be much chugging and popping before the potato was fired across the road to splat against the Corn Exchange, giving the driver (and any hapless passing pedestrian) an awful shock.

Edward Pawley died in 1966 after nearly twenty years as manager. Films ceased soon after in 1969 and the cinema went over to bingo. This, too, had closed by 1981; the building was demolished in 1984 and houses built on the site, the development being known as Regent Mews.

GROVE

CTE Cinema

The Grove CTE Cinema remains something of a mystery. *Kine Year Book* entries indicate that it was operating from 1948 until 1959. It is described as a 16mm 'static' cinema, suggesting that it was a permanent set-up in a small hall, 16mm being the narrower film gauge used in schools and hospitals, as well as for touring shows. No other details are given. The operators were CTE Cinemas of East St Helen's Street in Abingdon, the proprietors J. Thomas and R. Hobday. CTE ran four touring units in Berkshire, Buckinghamshire and Oxfordshire, as well as manufacturing arcs and projectors that were delightfully classified in the trade as 'sub-standard equipment', meaning in this case not for full-size 35mm film. The company also ran another 16mm CTE Cinema at Aldermaston, Berkshire, and the Cinema Royal (35mm) at Tadley in Hampshire.

Enquiries of long-time residents and local historians have failed to turn up any reference to, or memory of, the CTE in Grove itself. However, Grove airfield had a number of buildings and, although there was certainly no cinema when the Americans were using it during the war, it passed to the RAF immediately after. A possible explanation is that CTE contracted to operate a cinema in a Nissen hut or similar, as the dates certainly fit in with the RAF tenure. The airfield is no longer there, most of the land having been returned to agricultural use.

HENLEY-ON-THAMES

New Theatre/St Mary's Hall/Kenton Hall/Playhouse/New Playhouse/Kenton Theatre

The Kenton Theatre has had a chequered history since it opened back in November 1805 as the New Theatre with *School of Reform or How to Rule a Husband*. The Theatres' Trust *Guide to British Theatres* describes the building as 'domestic neo-Georgian style auditorium' behind a Georgian frontage; the building is the subject of a fascinating book, *The Well-Trod Stage* by Bill Port, which details its history and programmes over the past 200 years. The original design and erection was by William Parker, a Henley builder, with decoration designed and supervised by Mr Mortram of the Theatre Royal, Drury Lane in London.

During the theatre's period as St Mary's Hall, the first recorded film shown was on 15 November 1897 when Queen Victoria's Diamond Jubilee Procession Animated Photos shared the bill with the catchily named 'Lieut. Walter Cole and his Merry Folks and Refined Comic Concert and Operetta Company'.

Visits from other companies occurred in 1900 (C. Goodwin Norton, G. Edgerton and W.H. Speer's Grand Cinematograph and Variety Entertainment). 1901 attractions included Southsea photographer Alfred West's famous production *West's Our Navy*. This immensely popular show was based at the Polytechnic in London for fourteen years as well as touring Britain and the Empire. His pictures had the backing of the navy (and had been shown to Queen Victoria herself

Above and below: Two views of the Kenton Theatre, Henley-on-Thames, 2007. As well as the festoon rising curtain, the theatre also has conventional tabs. (IM, courtesy of Kenton Theatre)

at Osborne House – she was impressed). Finally, Dr Seaton's Grand National Animated Photos were on the bill for the last use of the (by then) Kenton Hall as a theatre. For the next sixteen years it served as a schoolroom.

Having made such an early contribution to popularising film, the Kenton Theatre came into its own again in 1988 when it hosted an evening called 'A Summer in the South' for the Save the Regal Fund. Sadly, as we shall see, the Regal was doomed, but in 1989 the Kenton showed the first in its film series, *A Fish Called Wanda*, from 20–26 January, using equipment donated by Gordon Mintern, former manager of the closed cinema.

Films were a regular part of the programming during the 1990s, clearly helping the theatre's finances during the period when there was no full-time cinema. It operates today predominantly as a live (mostly amateur) theatre, but held regular film showings up to 2006. These no longer take place because of dwindling audiences, but the ex-Regal Westrex projector with Peerless Xenon conversion and a modified tower is still in place and available for private hirings. The current seating capacity of the Kenton is 235.

The Picture Palace, Henley-on-Thames, in 1935. It closed the next year to make way for the Regal. (OCCPA)

Henley Picture Palace/Picture House/Palace/New Palace

Henley's first permanent home for pictures began life as a corrugated-iron roofed roller skating rink. The proprietor was F. Ellis, who also operated a cycle cleaning, re-enamelling and re-plating service from the premises at 33-35 Bell Street. During the winter skating season of 1910, he and two partners, Messrs Wilkins and Ring, were working on alterations to enable the premises to open as a picture house.

Having inspected the work, the town council were very concerned about the possibility of fire (that month, two picture palace fires were reported in the local papers, although neither had taken place in the area). They recommended that an inflammable erection connecting the rink to a private house be removed and that wooden partitions in the open yard be replaced at once with an iron fence. Two main steel girders had been fixed across the yard and the council recommended that Mr Ellis be allowed to erect on them 'an entirely non-inflammable building which shall only project six feet as measured from the main end wall of the rink for the purposes of the cinematograph apparatus'. *The Henley Chronicle* unfortunately mistook this latter point, reporting that the projection room should be an entirely *inflammable* building!

The Henley Picture Palace advertised that it was in operation only a week later (9 June 1911), showing every evening at 7 p.m. with matinees on Monday, Wednesday, Thursday and Saturday. There were programme changes twice a week, prices were 3d, 6d and 1s, and the performances were continuous. Although neither Henley paper graced the opening with an editorial mention, the advertisement claimed the new show was 'THE TALK OF HENLEY!'

It was certainly the talk of the neighbours, one of whom the very next week obtained an injunction against the proprietors for causing a serious nuisance and potential damage to his premises by the vibration from an engine and dynamo used to provide power. The complainant was Mr G.T. Savage, who ran an upholstery business next door. The theatre closed to undertake the necessary changes, reopening as Henley Picture House on 30 June. Shows in the 550-seat theatre included vaudeville and variety as well as pictures.

In June 1929 the building was modernised and became the New Palace Cinema, under the manager Mr E.W. Jeffs. The entrance had been remodelled with 30ft of glass doorways with a flashing sign over them. A new balcony was provided and an orchestra was under the direction of Miss Florence Rodger, late conductor of the Queen's Super Cinema, Dundee. Western Electric sound was installed the next year, but the new proprietors, Consolidated Cinematograph Theatres Ltd, soon decided that something better was needed for Henley, closing the Palace in 1936 for the construction of what was to become the Regal.

Regal/Odeon

Meanwhile, a company called Regal (Henley) Ltd had put forward a plan to build a cinema in Hart Street, which raised considerable controversy because it involved demolition or major alteration of a Georgian residence.

In January 1937 it was announced that Regal (Henley) Ltd had purchased the cinema being constructed in Bell Street from the Consolidated Cinematograph Co., thus saving the threatened house in Hart Street – an apparently happy solution for all. The Regal was erected on the site of the old Picture House with additional land previously occupied by Messrs Champion & Co.

Set back from the line of frontage of the street, the exterior was designed along Georgian lines by the architect L.T. (or Arthur F.) Hunt – reports vary – in order to blend in with the surroundings. If the exterior was period, the interior was 'in the modern abstract style carried out in a restrained manner. Harmonious blending of green, fawn and cream is the general interior colour scheme … and soft indirect lighting'. The cinema had 941 seats and a 15ft stage. A well-appointed café-restaurant was open daily from 10 a.m. to 10.30 p.m.

Left: The Regal, Henley-on-Thames. The destruction of the cinema in the 1993 followed a long campaign to save it. (CTA/John D. Sharp)

Below: The Regal, Henley, operated under the Odeon banner between 1945 and 1959. This was the last advertisement before it reverted to its old name of Regal.

ODEON

HENLEY
PHONE HENLEY-ON-THAMES 606
FREE CAR PARK

SUNDAY, March 15th	**Doors open 4.45 Last house 6.40**
Kirk Douglas Elsa Martinelli Walter Matthau	Richard Egan Dawn Addams Patric Knowles
in **The Indian Fighter**	in **KHYBER PATROL**
(U) CinemaScope Technicolor 5.15 8.10	(U) Colour 6.40
MONDAY, March 16th for 3 days	**Doors open 2.20 Last house 7.20**
JERRY LEWIS in	JACKIE LOUGHERY EDWARD KEMMER
THE GEISHA BOY in	**THE HOT ANGEL**
(U) Technicolor VistaVision 2.40 5.45 8.50	(U) 4.15 7.20
THURSDAY, March 19th for 3 days	**Doors open 1.55 Last house 7.10**
JOHN MILLS CECIL PARKER MICHAEL HORDERN	FRANK LOVEJOY in
in **I WAS MONTY'S DOUBLE**	**Cole Younger—Gunfighter**
2.15 5.30 8.45 (A)	CinemaScope (U) 3.55 7.10

SATURDAY, MARCH 14th—Boys' and Girls' Club		
Van Heflin in **SOUTH of ALGIERS**	Adventures of SGTS. DOUBLEDAY & AMES Episode 7	Also Interest and Cartoon

The Regal with organ console raised. (CTA/Tony Moss Collection/John D. Sharp)

The Regal opened quite literally to a fanfare on 14 May 1937, provided in this case by the trumpeters of the band of the Royal Artillery who played music before and at the ceremony. The opening was performed by the mayor, Councillor J.E. Chalcraft JP, who joked, 'It is said that Henley goes to sleep for 51 weeks of the year and wakes up only for the Royal Regatta. No doubt the new cinema will go a long way to dispose of that saying.' Amongst the dignitaries were representatives of what was described as the joint management, the proprietors Regal (Henley) Ltd and the controllers, County Cinemas Ltd, whose managing director C.J. Donada was present.

The opening programme was *Take My Tip* starring Jack Hulbert and Cicely Courtneidge, supported by a Disney Silly Symphony cartoon, *Mother Pluto*, Buster Keaton in *The Chemist* and the full Coronation Newsreel.

Odeon had gained a controlling interest in the company that ran the County circuit in May 1937, the same month as the Regal opened. The two circuits continued to be run fairly independently, however, until the start of the war when Odeon took over County's booking and accounts in August 1939. These functions were based very nearby, at Marlow and Cookham, just over the county border in Buckinghamshire. The Regal was renamed Odeon in 1945; the Rank Organisation withdrew from Henley on 21 March 1959 (the last film as the Odeon was *I Was Monty's Double*), but the cinema continued to be operated by an independent without a break, reverting to its original name from 22 March.

The new owners, Henley Picture House, took good care of their cinema and improved the facilities, the café being converted to a licensed bar in 1972. The same year, Henley and District Organ Trust installed the Compton three-manual, seven-unit organ from the Ritz/Essoldo in Tunbridge Wells; an organ lift and illuminated surround were added in 1975. The inaugural recital was by Reginald Dixon and the organ was played at monthly concerts until the cinema closed.

Sadly, the value of the Henley site attracted developers, and the Regal was subjected to a long and tenacious siege from neighbouring Waitrose, who wished to build a larger supermarket. The Henley area has always been home to influential public figures, and in this case they came out in force. The Save the Regal Trust launched a vigorous campaign, supported by a positive galaxy of star names with local connections including George Harrison, George Cole, Mary Hopkin, Joe Brown, John Mortimer and Sheridan Morley. The last of these remembered being taken to the Regal to see *Bambi* by his grandmother, actress Gladys Cooper ('OAP?', asked the cashier. 'No, I always sit in the circle', answered Gladys).

The cinema closed without warning after the show on 29 May 1986, not opening for business the next day when, ironically, the advertised feature was *Back to the Future*. Final capacity was 750 seats.

The battle raged on, the Trust being prepared to buy the Regal for its value as a cinema (around £200,000 at the time). A detailed plan for the development of the building was put forward, including two screens (with 200 and 400 seats) that, unusually, could be combined into a single large cinema or theatre auditorium of 740 seats when required. There would be a café, bar/restaurant and exhibition area, and the Compton organ would be retained. The British Film Institute (BFI) enthusiastically commended the scheme to the local council and the Trust pointed out that Henley Picture House Ltd would still make a considerable gain if Waitrose built on the car park rather than demolishing the cinema. Waitrose and South Oxfordshire District Council, on the other hand, argued that any total capacity in excess of 250 seats would be unviable as a cinema. On this latter aspect, the Trust and BFI were clearly more in tune with the business economics of running small cinemas.

In the end, the council, acting in the face of prolonged and massive support for the Regal's retention from Henley residents, agreed to the demolition of this fine art deco cinema. The Trust met for the last time in December 1993 as the bulldozers moved in, passing the resolution, 'In light of the destruction of the Regal Cinema by Waitrose, supported by the district council, the activities of the Save the Regal Trust are wound up with immediate effect.'

On a happier note, the organ had been removed in 1993 just before demolition. After a full restoration and enlargement, it is now in the Burtey Fen Collection in Pinchbeck, Lincolnshire, where it is regularly played to sell-out audiences and has been featured on CDs by top names from the organ world. Some of the projection and other equipment went to the Kenton Theatre. Archaeological work on the site revealed evidence of society in Henley dating back as far as the thirteenth century, six different levels of Bell Street being uncovered.

Regal/Regal Picturehouse

Waitrose had, as part of its planning application, proposed replacing the Regal with two studio cinemas, but as the planning battle and its aftermath wore on, considerable doubts were expressed about finding an operator. Following suggestions from prospective exhibitors, the plans were redrawn in 1994 with a smaller bar and refreshment area, allowing a third screen to be squeezed in, but it was not until 1996 that building work started in Boroma Way, close to, but not on, the site of the original Regal. Henley Town Council had offered a £200,000 grants and loans package to ensure the cinema went ahead.

Tony Kirkthorpe, director of the new operators, Metro Cinemas, promised that the new Regal would be a class above others in the area. 'Our cinema will be fully carpeted, the backs of chairs will be covered in material and not plastic, and drinks will be in bottles and glasses, not cartons. It should be a pleasant experience.' Film booking policy would be both mainstream and arthouse.

The Regal Picturehouse, Henley-on-Thames, celebrates its tenth birthday in February 2007. (IM)

One of the three screens in the Regal Picturehouse. (IM)

The long-awaited opening came with a gala première of *The Crucible* on 26 February 1997 and the cinema opened to the general public from 28 February. Metro Tartan Distribution ran the Regal (their only cinema) until December 2006, when it was taken over by City Screen (Picturehouse Cinemas) and renamed the Regal Picturehouse. The three auditoria of this comfortable little cinema seat 152, 101 and 85, and there is a licensed bar. Projection is by three Westar projectors with platters, all with DTS sound.

KIDLINGTON

Sterling

The Sterling, which opened in the High Street on 17 October 1938 with *I See Ice* starring George Formby, was a truly enormous cinema for a village that was close to, although separate from, Oxford. The opening ceremony was performed by Councillor W.A. Cattell, assisted by Councillors Frank Wise and A.H. Calcutt. The Sterling boasted 908 seats (the population of Kidlington was given as only 1,073 in the *Kine Year Book* for 1939, rising to 3,100 in the 1943 edition!), a 30ft proscenium and a café. Prices ranged from 6d to 2s. The promoters had based their capacity on the imminent expansion of Kidlington with the planned Garden City, but the war started when only the first phase had been completed. The proprietors were Sterling Entertainments Ltd of 31 Market Square, Witney, which was the address of the Palace Cinema. The Sterling was operated by Ernest Huddleston from his very successful Witney base.

Contemporary photographs show the sleek lines of the interior, clearly modelled on the modern large city centre cinemas of the time. An unusual feature was the position of the projection room in the balcony 'void' rather than the more common location above the rear of the balcony; this gave a virtually level throw, eliminating the 'keystone' effect often experienced in larger cinemas because of the acute angle of projection. Removable panels at the back of the balcony covered large windows in the frontage of the building, which could be opened for ventilation, an important consideration when patrons were able to smoke during the show.

In the first year, deputy manager Kathleen Hawken recalled only ten or twenty people turning up each evening. But when the airport was taken over to train pilots, the audiences started to grow and the cinema was often filled to capacity. The restaurant also proved popular, and there were dances, a pantomime with local people and fundraising for the war effort. The power used to fail quite often, so Mr Huddleston installed a pianola (playing from paper rolls) on the stage to keep the audience entertained. After one session of pedalling away in the dark, Kathleen Hawken was told by an acquaintance, 'I didn't know you could play as well as that'!

Films were continuous from 6 p.m. daily with, unlike at Witney, a show on Sunday. Ernest Huddleston was succeeded in the business by his son Lawrence, who struggled to operate such a large building against the lure of nearby Oxford city centre and improving public and private transport. Attendances were often below 100 and, impressive though the auditorium was with a good audience, it felt cheerless when you were only one of a handful. Changes over the years had included the introduction of British Thomson-Houston SUPA projectors, massive machines incorporating all the elements of projection equipment into one single case. The café had been turned into a licensed bar, rather bizarrely called the Disney Bar and with a ceiling mural of cartoon characters.

Only 100 attended the final performance, a matinee showing of Patrick Wayne in *The People that Time Forgot* on 31 December 1977. Lawrence Huddleston said that it had been uneconomic for years, 'but I can't afford to keep it open any longer. I don't like to see it close, but it just can't keep going'. The manager at the time of the closure was Cyril Hawken, who had taken

Above and below: The Sterling, Kidlington. The top windows over the foyer were for ventilation as the projection room was located in the 'wedge' of the balcony void. (OCCPA)

The Sterling in 2000, still very recognisable despite being a supermarket for many years. (IM)

over just two months after the cinema opened; he was over seventy and Lawrence Huddleston was sixty-eight.

Bovis Construction won the contract to carry out a £0.5 million conversion into a supermarket for Tesco, which still operates in 2007. No sign of its original purpose exists in the public areas inside the store, though the exterior frontage of the old Sterling is remarkably recognisable even after thirty years of trading as a supermarket.

MIDDLE BARTON

Premier/Palace

In 1924 farmers William and Eliza Constable arranged for a wooden building to be transported from Kent and set up at 106 North Street to be operated by their son Albert as the Premier Cinema. An engine provided power and a pianist supplied accompaniment and, although seated with wooden benches, the cinema was a popular attraction in this very rural area. In the 1920s and 1930s Robert Jarvis, the local bus proprietor, ran coaches from Wootton, Tackley and the Heyfords, with an inclusive price for ticket and entrance; the fish and chip shop next door was also popular with audiences. As well as cinema, the hall was used for drama, dances and wedding receptions.

The war intervened and the cinema was taken over by the army as sleeping quarters. During and immediately after the war, a Mr Sanders from Deddington gave film shows at the Mission Hall on Monday nights, with an admission price of 6d.

After the war, the cinema was reopened as the Palace by Jim Smith, the former landlord of the Jolly Boatman at Thrupp, and he and his wife made a number of improvements. A breeze-block structure was built around the wooden building and proper cinema seats were introduced on a sloping floor. They were arranged in three blocks, with a wide central row and two very narrow ones at the sides. The pay box at the front had doors leading in on either side of the screen, the projectors being at the end furthest away from the road.

In October 1954 Mr Smith put Middle Barton firmly on the Oxfordshire cinema map by being the first public cinema in the county to install Cinemascope, the new widescreen process introduced by Twentieth Century Fox in the fight-back against television. He had obtained the special lenses from Holland and had himself made the frame for the new screen measuring 16ft by 8ft, with flaps to close down to normal size when scope films were not available. This was the culmination of a £2,000 modernisation package and was a major coup for what then counted as a tiny cinema with only 206 seats, the smallest cinema in Europe to install Cinemascope at the time.

Even these improvements did not make for a totally pleasant film-going experience. Barbara Imbert and Jessie Newman remember going there well:

> The whole cinema was very damp and the plush seats soaked it up; people had to sit on the edge or bring their own cushions. During the interval, people used to bring in fish and chips and Jim Smith would say, 'Don't bring those smelly fish and chips in here unless there's some for me!' When there was a breakdown, he would apologise and say we were going to get *Gone with the Wind* soon – but we never did.

Mrs Smith kept an eye on unaccompanied children in the front rows, which she called 'babysitting for a bob'. The programmes were good value, consisting of two feature films, changing on Monday and Thursday. The cinema was closed on Wednesday and Saturday.

Like so many little family-run village and town cinemas, the Palace could not continue and closed in 1963. It was taken over for factory and office use by Steepletone; the building was named Cinema House, but externally was little changed. The end finally came in 1997 when it was demolished and replaced with two houses.

OXFORD

New Theatre / Apollo Theatre / New Theatre
Although never full-time cinemas, the various New Theatres in George Street have played their part in bringing film to Oxford audiences over the years. Most importantly, the second (1886) New Theatre on the site, designed by Drinkwater, was the venue for the first animated pictures in Oxford. These opened on Monday 7 September 1896 for the week, as part of a burlesque show *The Gay Princess or, a Trip to Happyland*.

W.G.R. Sprague, a leading theatre architect of the period whose remaining work is now highly cherished, remodelled the theatre in 1908. This 'New' also regularly presented animated pictures as part of its variety programmes; it was one of three halls in Oxford that showed the film of the 1911 Oxford and Cambridge boat race on the actual evening of the event (the others were the Castle Street Electric Theatre and the Jeune Street Picture Palace).

The Sprague theatre was completely demolished in February 1933 and the present theatre built in art-deco style for the Dorrill family, opening on 26 February 1934. The architects were W. & T.R. Milburn, with interior design by T.P. Bennett, and although designed as a live theatre

The Palace, Middle Barton (white building on left), the scene of Oxfordshire's first public presentation of Cinemascope. (The Bartons Local History Group)

The Palace, Middle Barton, seen from the air. A coach is parked alongside. (The Bartons Local History Group)

The Palace lived on as a factory after closure in 1963, but the shape of the building remained the same. (CTA/ Tony Moss Collection)

the follow-spot box could be used as a projection room if ever required. The call came on 21 November 1938 when the very first feature-length cartoon, Walt Disney's *Snow White and the Seven Dwarfs*, was presented. This extremely popular film enjoyed its exclusive first run in Oxford at the theatre; this was not so satisfactory from a technical viewpoint as the acute angle of projection led to a pronounced keystone distortion on the screen. The New reverted to live theatre immediately after, so it does not appear that this was intended as a general change of policy by the management, and might even have been a private letting to one of the cinema companies.

In 1972, the New Theatre became part of the Howard & Wyndham Group of theatres. They carved out part of the seating of the rear dress circle and built a new lighting control box and projection room, in which they installed two GK 21 projectors. These were used to project a Pearl & Dean advertisement reel onto the safety curtain during intervals (which caused protests during opera seasons as being unseemly for an opera house) and to present re-runs of feature films using a proper screen when no live shows were available. Films stopped in the 1980s although the advertisement reel was still being shown in the late 1990s. Since then, the sing-along version of *The Sound of Music* has been presented, but using back projection.

Subsequent operators have been Apollo Leisure (1977), SFX Entertainment (2000) and Clear Channel Entertainment (2001). When the theatre was restored by Clear Channel and reverted to its original name in September 2003, the projectors were removed although the control/ projection room remains.

East Oxford Constitutional Hall/Lyric Hall/Empire Theatre/East Oxford Theatre/ Hippodrome/Palace Picture Theatre/Palace Cinema

As its many names suggest, this building at 106/108 Cowley Road had a chequered career as an entertainment venue. Built by the Oxford Constitutional Hall Co. Ltd on the site of a former nursery bought from brewer George H. Morrell, the foundation stone was laid in 1889 by another brewer, Alexander William Hall, the local MP. The architect was Harry Wilkinson Moore and the construction is of brick with stone facings. The hall was fitted with a stage at the front and had a gallery running round the other three sides. It opened for lettings the next year and was used for lectures, concerts and amateur dramatics but, probably because of its political sponsorship, bookings were not as good as originally anticipated. It was decided to let the hall on a more long-term basis to a public entertainment concern.

In January 1898 it was renamed the Lyric Hall, with proprietor A.L. Baron who opened his season with J.W. Isham's Oriental America singing and dancing troupe. On 1 January 1900 travelling Velograph animated picture exhibitor Albany Ward took over as manager and licensee,

The New Theatre, Oxford regains its name in September 2003. The film projection equipment was removed at the time of this refurbishment. (IM)

changing the name to the Empire Theatre of Varieties. He presented plays, variety and regular Velograph pictures, which allows the Empire to lay claim to being the first permanent home of pictures in the city. An energetic entrepreneur, he also ran an entertainment booking agency and advertising business from the address; he lived 'above the shop' with his wife and mother-in-law. Albany Ward moved on to Weymouth in 1906 to found his circuit of west country cinemas and Frank Stuart, who also held the licence for the Elm Tree pub opposite, took over.

Stuart changed the name to the East Oxford Theatre and put in plans for additional gallery space. He continued the policy of plays, variety and pictures and, like Albany Ward, obviously saw that there was great potential in the new medium, for by 1910 he had put in plans for two buildings dedicated to pictures.

The East Oxford Theatre held a 'Benefit to Mr Frank Stuart' on Saturday 21 May 1910. The evening offered a 'monster programme. 6 hours' continuous entertainment'. This comprised animated pictures including all the latest subjects, dramatic episodes, singers, comedians, Leonard Moon's Merrymakers, a local child actress, an Indian club expert and concluded with a new and original Dramatic Festival by members of Mr and Mrs Stuart's Dramatic Co. Finally (and as the show started at 6 p.m. this would have been around midnight) 'Auld Lang Syne' concluded the extravaganza. Anyone who lasted the whole course would have dragged home feeling they had certainly had their money's worth, as usual prices applied.

Scott Alexander took control of the theatre from Frank Stuart on 14 November 1910 and, predictably, renamed the theatre the Oxford Hippodrome to mark his tenure. In 1912 the hall received a major 'reconstruction for cinematograph purposes', indicating that pictures were no longer an incidental part of the general programme. A better projection room was built and the old side galleries were replaced with a straight fireproof balcony more suited to films. The house was entirely redecorated and new tip-up seats introduced. The programme was still 'partly cinematography and partly varieties', with two performances nightly and a special children's matinee on Saturday afternoons. Prices were set to 'allow all classes to enjoy a high-class entertainment at a reasonable cost'. The building was renamed the Palace Theatre and reopened for business on 14 October 1912 with a programme of pictures and variety. Films were the usual mix of drama, comedy and 'interest'.

Films gradually took over from variety and the Palace continued as a cinema, the location of a dance hall below, with the inevitable seepage of sound no doubt adding to the experience of cinema-going above!

In 1921 a two-manual 'straight organ' (i.e. a church rather than cinema-type) was introduced to complement a trio of musicians. It was removed with the installation of Western Electric sound in 1930 and sold back to George Jackson, the original builder. Other changes in this period included cutting back the stage-line to allow more stalls seats and the building of a new projection room.

The Palace was taken over by Union Cinemas in 1932 and passed to ABC in 1937; it closed as a cinema on 4 June 1938 with the end of a three-day run of Bing Crosby in *Double or Nothing* paired with *The Last Adventurers*. By this point, the old building was way below what was expected from a cinema and the opening of the luxurious Regal further up Cowley Road must have been the final straw. Photographs taken by Union in the early 1930s show an old, rather bleak hall with an open pitched roof with exposed metal trusses, looking very like it did more than twenty years before when it was first remodelled for films.

The building has survived and was used for fifty-five years by Blackwell's Publishing until they moved out in 2005. The frontage is still easily comparable to old photographs and the outline of the fly tower is instantly recognisable to theatre buffs. Internal floors and partitions have removed most theatrical features, although wooden features over bricked-in exit doors and the original curving stairs to the balcony remain. Remains of the theatre and scenery handling equipment

The Palace, Cowley Road. This was Albany
Ward's theatre when he settled in Oxford in
1900. The interior was very dated by the time
this picture was taken by Union in the early
1930s. (CTA)

The Palace, Cowley Road, 2000. The
frontage is still recognisable, and the
body of the auditorium, with flytower, is
unmistakable. (IM)

remained above the false ceiling of the upper floor. The manager's office and flat still survive at the front and, like in any self-respecting former theatre, are said to have an atmosphere which has made some uneasy! Seating capacity at closure was listed as 591, having been as high as 650 in 1915.

Oxford Electric Theatre/Picture House (Castle Street)

Oxford's first building dedicated solely to pictures was in Castle Street and was opened by Frank Stuart on 16 November 1910, two days after his successor as licensee of the East Oxford Theatre had taken over there.

Originally the site of the Oxford University and City Baths and Wash Houses (hence, presumably, the name of the alley down the right-hand side, Bath Court), the building was reconstructed as a shop and workshop in 1908. In October 1910 architect John R. Wilkins of Oxford submitted plans for a 'slight alteration to an existing building'. The workshop on the left-hand side became an entrance hall, with pay desk and doors leading into the side of the auditorium. The screen was at the street end, with exits each side leading out into Castle Street. The tiny auditorium was L-shaped, with eighteen rows of benches or seats provided (ten rows 15ft wide, narrowing to around 7 or 8ft). The actual number seated was not recorded at this stage.

The original plans show a small operating room (off centre) over the back two rows of seats. It has been suggested that the rewinding room was at the other end of the cinema, causing the highly combustible reels of nitrate film to be carried through the audience. This is not apparent from the plans, but if true was a very dangerous practice.

The proprietorship of the Electric Theatre changed hands in 1912, the managing partner being a Mr Froude. The new management (Castle Street Picturedrome Company (Oxford) Ltd) enlarged the premises – how is not specified and no plans are on file – thoroughly redecorated and upholstered the interior with 'no expense being spared to ensure the comfort of patrons'. There was now seating for 250 and, unlike other shows in Oxford, the Electric gave separate rather than continuous performances, each lasting just over an hour. There were two performances nightly, with three regular shows and two children's matinees on Saturdays. In a feature on the Electric, which appeared in the *Oxford Journal Illustrated* on 20 March 1912, a special point was made that the films for these matinees were specially chosen not only to amuse but to be of real educational value. It is interesting that this was underlined by the management, as often the children's matinees of the time were made up of part of the normal programme and this was causing great concern nationally as to the suitability of the films shown.

The Electric Theatre seldom advertised in the papers, relying on local clientele; it ran on until around 1923 by which time it was very small and old-fashioned compared with its rivals. The last proprietor was Malcolm Hamlet, whose manager was L.J. Belchman. There were two changes of programme weekly; prices were from 5d to 1s and seating was provided for 200.

Oxford's first real cinema found a new life as a canteen for the employees of Cooper's store and from 1939 to 1968 was a canteen for Oxfordshire County Council staff, after which it was demolished to make way for the Westgate Centre.

(East Oxford) Picture Palace/Penultimate Picture Palace/Ultimate Picture Palace

As well as converting the Castle Street premises in 1910, Frank Stuart had commissioned his architect John Wilkins to design a completely new building, the Picture Palace in Jeune Street, off Cowley Road. The location was beside Stuart's Elm Tree tavern and almost opposite his old East Oxford Theatre which was at this point known as the Hippodrome on live shows but would soon become the Palace Cinema. The builders were Kingerlee of Oxford.

The Oxford Electric Theatre in Castle Street opened in 1910. This detail from a photograph by Harry Minn is the only known surviving picture of Oxford's first cinema. (Bodleian Library – see acknowledgments for full details)

The single-floor hall opened for a private view on the afternoon of 24 February 1911, and to the public the next day. It was of very basic design, being a brick-built hall behind a show front proclaiming 'Oxford Picture Palace Limited'. There was a pavement paybox with entrances to the auditorium each side and a miniscule box for the operator was reached up a ladder from the back of the pay booth. The interior decoration was in red and white.

The *Oxford Journal Illustrated* visited soon after the opening and was fulsome in its praise in a full-page article 'The Cinematograph as Entertainment':

Mr Stuart claims for the East Oxford Picture Palace that it is one of the best appointed in the provinces. It certainly excels in design, general dimensions, and in personal comfort many of the popular houses in the heart of London. The interior of the Picture Palace is spacious and designed especially for the comfort of the visitors. There is ample seating accommodation for 400 at each performance, tip-up fauteils being provided, as in the highest class theatres, for the highest priced seats. The floor is of parquet, dry, warm and comfortable, and an equable temperature, without draughts, is provided by six radiators.

The article goes on to praise the ventilation, fire precautions and the fireproof nature and location of the single 'cinematograph machine' in use. The throw to the screen was 54ft. Programmes changed three times weekly and there were three shows nightly (each lasting about an hour) with two children's afternoon matinees on Saturdays.

One notable omission (not mentioned in the eulogy) was the lack of toilets within the theatre. This was because of the joint ownership with The Elms next door, and a door on the right towards the bottom of the hall led into the yard where the pub's lavatories were situated. Ken Scroggs vividly remembered going to the Picture Palace as a boy and recollected that if the film was at an exciting point children didn't always bother going out. The atmosphere in the front rows could be unpleasant!

The Picture Palace (sometimes referred to as the East Oxford Picture Palace) did not advertise in the press regularly, no doubt relying on word of mouth and passing trade. The exact closing date is unknown but is thought to have been between 1918 and 1920. The old cinema was gutted by Cullens of Didcot and the old projector apparently inspired them to branch into the cinema business and open the Coronet in their home town. Remarkably, the Picture Palace escaped development and was used for storage for many years; on a personal note I remember seeing the doors standing open as I drove past in the mid-1970s and being allowed in. The building was filled with furniture and divided along its length by a light partition; there were windows in the left-hand wall. The remains of the old screen were still there and it was possible to clamber up the iron ladder into the original tiny operating box.

Another visitor to this cinematic Rip Van Winkle was lawyer Bill Heine who had the vision to reopen the cinema as the Penultimate Picture Palace (PPP). The name came from a bank manager who said that, if not the ultimate in bad ideas, it was certainly the penultimate! The planners gave permission for a return to cinema use in 1974 and Bill Heine proceeded to convert the 1911 structure into a cinema fit for the 1970s. A major problem was building toilets without reducing capacity and he personally excavated an area at the front below the screen. A new projection room was provided, extending the full width of the entrance area, but because of roof levels periscope projection had to be used, losing light and definition. Seating was for 184; it is difficult to imagine the squeeze in the hall with its original capacity of 400, even with benches.

The frontage remained structurally unaltered, with the original entrances and pay box. It was painted black with a striking sculpture of Al Jolson based on *The Jazz Singer*. The door handles were Mae West's lips and there were no sweets, no music unless it was live and no

This page: Three views of the Picture Palace, Jeune Street: closed in the 1950s, as the Penultimate Picture Palace in the 1980s and as the Ultimate Picture Palace in 2006. (OCCPA, CTA, IM). See also page 14.

The simple, plain auditorium of the Ultimate Picture Palace, 2006. (IM)

smoking (an innovative move at the time). Neither was there screen advertising but the toilets were mischievously marked *Pearl* and *Dean*. The cinema was reopened by Bill Heine and Pablo Butcher after its fifty-year sleep on 18 July 1976 with *Winstanley*.

The cinema was very successful in its early days, with annual admissions around the 100,000 mark. 'We sometimes turn away more people than we let in. We set out to raise the quality and lower the price, aiming for high turnover and maximum seat uptake', Bill Heine said in a 1978 interview. At 50p, admission was less than half the price of the city centre opposition. He considered installing a balcony to increase capacity and a new projection room was built forward of the extended 1976 one, in order to enable direct rather than periscope projection. The equipment consisted of two Westar 3 projectors on Kalee stands with 2,000ft changeovers, BT-H xenon lamphouses and RCA sound.

Sadly, the PPP became better known for legal and planning wrangles and in 1979 changed to a private club to get round restrictions on late-night opening following a campaign by local residents. Other problems included legal action by Stanley Kubrick to prevent his withdrawn film *A Clockwork Orange* being shown in 1988. On 16 March 1994 the PPP closed with *Cinema Paradiso* and in July the Penultimate Picture Co. went into liquidation.

There was more drama to come. Whilst the owners, the Donnington Hospital Trust, were talking to businessmen interested in taking over the closed cinema, the Oxford Freedom Network occupied the building, partly as a protest against the forcible eviction of squatters from a disused nurses' home elsewhere in Oxford. They re-christened it 'Section 6 Cinema' and in August and September 1994 mounted free film shows using video including a children's matinee of *Aladdin* and the *Star Wars* trilogy. (Section 6 was a reference to part of the 1977 Criminal Law Act which made squatting legal.)

Finally, after the building was reclaimed, The Last Picture Show Ltd sought planning permission to reconstruct the frontage. Brothers Saied and Zaid Marham spent £40,000 restoring and opening the cinema on a twenty-five-year lease. The frontage had to be virtually rebuilt, replacing a rotting steel support beam and restoring the classical features of the original. Gone was the gothic black, which was replaced with ivory, features being picked out in rose red and grey, revealing the detail of the attractive frontage for the first time for many years. Now named the Ultimate Picture Palace, it reopened on 4 June 1996 with the director's cut of *Blade Runner*. The current projection kit consists of a single Westar with tower, Dolby sound and a BT-H xenon lamphouse.

Saied Marham has spent most of his working life at the PPP/UPP as cashier, usher and now manager/proprietor. The Oxford Picture Palace lives on under his care – a unique survival that is very much the same as when it opened in 1911. The building is now Grade II listed.

Electra Palace / Electra

The next cinema to be built in Oxford was the Electra Palace in Queen Street. The architects were Homer and Lucas and the builders Messrs T.H. Kingerlee & Sons, who had just finished the Picture Palace. With plans approved on 27 January 1911, up to sixty workmen toiled day and night for six weeks to construct the building on the former site of Prior and Rickard, a house furnishers.

The Electra was in a different class to its two little predecessors, costing £3,000 to build. The entrance was in pure white with a marble tessellated floor. Seating was for 500, and the tip-up seats, upholstered in red plush (the best seats had armrests as well) were on a steeply raked floor so that everyone could see the screen without obstruction. The walls had light oak coloured panels.

The L-shaped auditorium was unusual, being set back from the road and twice as wide as the frontage, the cinema having been constructed beside and behind its next door neighbour, the Maypole Dairy. The rather narrow entrance therefore belied the size of the hall one entered, having passed through a handsome lounge waiting area. A brick-built fireproof operating room was built completely outside the hall and was equipped with two Empire No. 12 machines so that there would be no breaks between reels.

The opening was on 25 March 1911 and 700 guests were invited to a lavish event, palms and plants suitable to the occasion being specially brought in. The fact that there were so many more guests than seats may have led to one unfortunate gentleman first sitting on a lady's lap, and then on moving missing the seat altogether and sitting down on the floor! An attendant with an electric torch – another innovation – rescued him before he could cause further mayhem.

Performances were continuous from 2 to 10.30 p.m. with patrons being able to come and go as they pleased. Music was provided; the Electra Orchestra, under cellist Archie Payne gained quite a reputation locally and gave charity performances elsewhere including at the Grand, Abingdon. Prices were 3d, 6d and 1s, a good deal dearer than those of the competitors at the time. The programmes consisted of the usual fare of comedy, drama, interest and news with a special programme for children's matinees.

Business was good and in 1913 the Maypole Dairy was incorporated into the cinema building, doubling the frontage. Around 118 additional seats were added on the left-hand side at the back and a new projection room was built over the back of the auditorium. Further extensions took place around 1920, at which point the shallow balcony must have been added, as it does not appear in the original plans or those of the 1913 extension. In 1931 the Electra fitted the Western Electric sound system, opening on 9 February with *Almost a Honeymoon*, the first night featuring a personal appearance by the stars, Donald Calthorp and Dodo Watts. Shortly after, the ownership changed from Electra Palace Co. (Oxford) Ltd to Union Cinemas. Prices were 9d to 3s and a café was advertised. By this point the Electra had 1,200 seats, a great increase on the original 500. 1937 saw the transfer of Union to ABC, who reduced seating to 1,078. By the 1950s the Electra was somewhat outdated and was the last cinema to go over to Cinemascope. ABC was clearly getting ready to divest itself of one of its three city centre cinemas and the old Electra, in its valuable position in a main shopping street, was the obvious choice. The end came on 23 August 1958 with Errol Flynn and Dorothy Malone in *Too Much, Too Soon*.

The old cinema was split horizontally and became a Co-Op department store. The segmented barrel-vaulted roof of the main auditorium was retained and formed the ceiling of the upstairs floor of the shop. Eventually the Co-Op moved out and the cinema that had set new standards of luxury back in 1911 was totally demolished in 1978 to make way for the current Marks & Spencer store.

Left and opposite: The Electra, Queen Street, Oxford; the frontage and the awkward L-shaped auditorium are seen in the 1930s. The balcony had been added by this stage. (CTA)

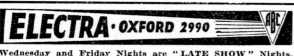

ELECTRA · OXFORD 2990

Wednesday and Friday Nights are " LATE SHOW " Nights.
Progs. Start Later—End Later (11 p.m. approx.). See Times

Monday, August 18th: 3 Days Last Prog. 6.55 (Wed. 7.40)	Thursday, Aug. 21st: 3 Days Last Prog. 6.35 (Fri. 7.20)
John Agar June Kenny **SIX INCHES TALL** 2.20, 5.35, 8.50 (A) (Wed. 3.05, 6.20, 9.35)	Errol Flynn Dorothy Malone **TOO MUCH, TOO SOON** 1.10, 4.45, 8.25 (A) (Fri. 1.55, 5.30, 9.10)
Yvonne Lime Gary Clarke **THE RECKLESS AGE** 3.50, 7.05 (Wed. 4.35, 7.50) (A)	Clint Walker Virginia Mayo **FORT DOBBS** 2.55, 6.35, (Fri. 3.40, 7.20) (U)

Sunday, Aug. 17th: (1 Day Only) Cont. 4 p.m. Last Prog. 6.50
Jeff Chandler, Maureen O'Hara, **WAR ARROW** Tech. (U)
Cornel Wilde, Richard Conte, **THE BIG COMBO** (A)

The final programme at the Electra came on 23 August 1958 but the building lived on as a Co-Op store for many years.

Cinematograph Theatre / George Street Cinema

Lisemore's Stores in George Street was demolished in 1911 for yet another cinema building project in this extremely busy period; the Oxford Cinematograph Theatre Co. (H.G. Wilson, resident manager) were the proprietors and the architect was Gilbert W. Booth of London. The Cinematograph Theatre was at 32 George Street (the name was later changed to George Street Cinema) and opened on Saturday 23 March 1912. The opening ceremony was performed by the member of parliament for Oxford City, Viscount Valentia C.B. at a private viewing in the afternoon; the first public performance was held that evening at 6 p.m. with the proceeds in aid of charity.

A single-floored auditorium ran lengthways along George Street, with the street entrance at the right-hand end. Seating was for 608 with three blocks and two gangways. As at the Electra two projectors were installed, allowing for continuous shows, with the projection room built high up over the entrance and entirely separated from the auditorium A decorative scenic dado ran round the top of the walls, similar in style to that of the Abingdon Pavilion.

Oxford Journal Illustrated visited and photographed the new picture theatre both inside and out. It was described as luxuriously fitted throughout with 'the most perfect system of ventilation' consisting of large electric fans in the roof giving a constant supply of fresh air, and with heating by radiators. An orchestra of four musicians was in residence.

Continuous performances were given daily from 2.30 to 10.30 p.m. with a complete change of programme on Mondays and Thursdays. Prices matched those of the nearby Electra at 1s, 6d and 3d.

The cinema closed on 5 April 1930 for extensive redecoration, reseating and the installation of Edibell sound apparatus, reopening with Ronald Colman in *Bulldog Drummond* on 21 April, Easter Monday. The Edibell system does not seem to have been satisfactory as the next year it had changed to the more popular Western Electric system. Union Cinemas had taken over both this cinema and the Super, and the last advertised programme, Ralph Lynn in *Dirty Work*, was on Saturday 30 March 1935. The cinema and adjacent buildings were immediately demolished to make way for the development of the new Union Ritz Cinema. The foyer of the Ritz (now the Odeon George Street) stands at the old screen end; a new road, Gloucester Street, through to Gloucester Green was created and a shop was built at the old entrance end. Although the

The Cinematograph Theatre/George Street Cinema, Oxford, opened in 1912. (Jeremy's of Oxford)

Oxford Cinematograph Theatre itself is no more, film entertainment has been presented on this site from 1912 right through to the present day.

North Oxford Kinema/(New) Scala/Studio 1 & 2, Studio 1 & X, Phoenix Picturehouse

The next development was in November 1912, when plans were submitted by R.H.J. Bartlett for a cinema in Walton Street. The architect was Gilbert T. Gardner of St Aldates, Oxford, who was responsible for other Oxford landmarks including the Cadena Café in Cornmarket and Headington Girls' School. His practice also designed the much larger Central Cinema in Reading. The builders were Ephraim Organ & Son, also from Oxford.

The North Oxford Kinema, which opened on Saturday 15 March 1913, was entered through an ornate entrance with pillars and decorative plasterwork, then through a foyer and a separate lounge area before reaching the auditorium. This long entrance was because the auditorium was wider than the frontage, the whole building having been fitted round the house next door. Ever conscious of the fire-related tragedies associated with early cinemas, the construction was of brick, with fireproof asbestos cement tiles. The 'lantern room' was situated above the auditorium, which consisted of 498 seats on a single floor, raked down to the screen in order to provide good sightlines.

Paul Marriott, in his booklet *Early Oxford Picture Palaces*, records the detailed memories of former projectionist Syd Taylor who went to the North Oxford Kinema as a boy in 1915:

> In comparison with the size of the auditorium, it had two spacious vestibules. The outer one had a full-size sweet shop (on the left of the entrance), with quite large windows dressed with all sorts of sweets, candies and chocolates. Next to the shop and on the left of the vestibule was

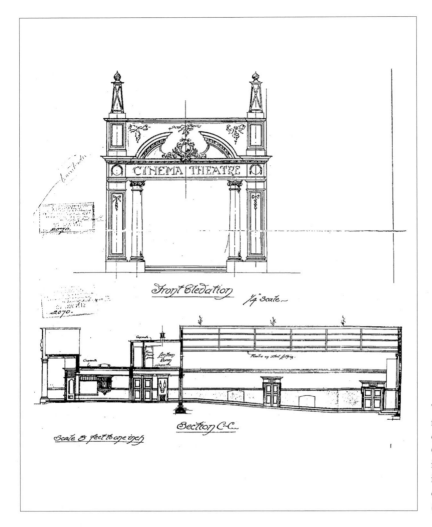

Front Elevation ¼" scale

Section C-C

Scale 8 feet to one inch

The ornate narrow frontage of the North Oxford Kinema in Walton Street is shown in the orginal plans. (OCCPA)

the cash desk. At the back and facing the street, were three sets of double doors through which one passed into the second vestibule, furnished with lounge suites, settee and two chairs all in wickerwork and cushioned.

All this grandeur led to the auditorium itself. A red plush curtain separated the little orchestra from the screen, which was in a pillared decorative surround. (This original scheme was still in place on the back wall behind the modern screen when the Star Group stripped out the auditorium for twinning in 1970 and traces still remain in 2007.)

Mr Bartlett and his fellow proprietors W. Beeson and C. Green were succeeded by H.T. Lambert who ran the N.O.K. for three years until 1920, when it was renamed the Scala when it came under the management of C.W. Poole's Entertainments, based in Gloucester. The Poole family were a household name, having toured the country with their spectacular Myriorama show. The cinematograph had played an increasingly important role in their shows and they were now developing their interests in running cinemas. After re-decoration and renovation they held a grand reopening on Monday 19 April 1920 with a three-day programme of Anita Stewart in *Virtuous Wives* supported by a Mutt and Jeff cartoon, *Pathé Topical Gazette* newsreel and a 'full programme of comedies'. There was a complete change of programme from Thursday. Prices were 1s 3d, 9d and 5d with a continuous performance from 5.30 to 10.30 p.m., Saturdays from 2.30. The Scala Orchestra were advertised as providing music throughout.

There then followed a series of owners in rapid succession. Walshaw Enterprises (lessee and resident manager G. WALker and general manager W. SHAW) are listed from 1923; amongst other innovations they filmed their own local newsreel, the *Scala Local Topical*. In 1925 a colourful character, cockney Ben Jay, took over. He was a showman through and through and, as the New Scala, he presented a full continuous programme of two feature films and supporting comedies, news and serial, operating from 2.15 p.m. The nine-piece orchestra under George Tugwood not only accompanied the silent films, but also presented a musical interlude with community singing of popular songs with the words projected onto the screen. Free tea and biscuits were provided at matinees, and Ben Jay would apparently cut or change the film during the performance in response to audience mood.

Unfortunately, this heady mixture of entertainment led to rowdy behaviour from undergraduates resulting in the withdrawal of the New Scala's university licence in 1927, meaning that students were no longer able to attend. Jay left Oxford and returned to London, where he set up and ran the Ben Jay circuit based at the Corner Cinema, Tottenham.

The next proprietor (1927) was J. Bailiff who listed his address as the Palace Cinema in Henley-on-Thames, but by the end of the year he, too, had handed over, this time to E.A. Roberts, who introduced the Panotrope system for amplifying gramophone records to accompany films. It seemed that the Scala was a difficult house to run successfully, but the next change was to a family firm who were to run the cinema for the next forty years.

J. 'Jackie' Edward Poyntz already ran the Olney Electric Cinema in Buckinghamshire. He took the Scala over in June 1930 and one of his daughters continued to run Olney on his behalf until around 1946. He booked both cinemas from Oxford where he installed BT-H sound, the first talkie being the musical *Happy Days*. In 1939 Poyntz embarked on a major reconstruction of the frontage, taking in the house next door so that the street aspect was the same width as the auditorium, which was now extended to house 575 seats. He was only allowed to complete this work on the outbreak of war because the old frontage had already been ripped off!

The new front was, like the new management, plain and understated in style. There was no longer a sweetshop, as Mr Poyntz believed people should be able to watch a film in peace (he would be horrified at the popcorn and fizzy-drink ridden multiplexes of today). After Mr Poyntz's retirement the business was taken over by his son-in-law and daughter, Eric and Maisie Bowtell, and another daughter, Daphne Poyntz.

The only exterior advertising consisted of a few stills in the windowpanes of the doors, to the extent that when I came to Oxford in 1967 and walked down Walton Street for the first time one morning I initially thought that it was a closed cinema! Once inside, however, it was clear that all the attention was on the choice and presentation of the programme. Operating as an art house, public programmes were presented from Monday to Saturday only, with the Oxford Film Society meeting there on Sundays – one of relatively few at the time to offer 35mm presentation to their members.

The Scala developed a highly successful policy of programming specialist and foreign films (the latter always in the original and subtitled, never dubbed), with mainstream and classic re-runs during university vacations. Projection was by BT-H SUPA Mark II projectors, and these were fitted with xenon lamphouses (unusual when carbon arcs were the norm but now, of course, universal) and automatic changeovers – the only cinema in the county to offer

As the Scala, the Walton Street cinema had a strong reputation for foreign films. This picture was taken in 1970 just after Star took over. (IM)

this degree of sophistication. There were also three sets of lenses for each projector, enabling the old Academy ratio, widescreen and cinemascope films to be presented in their correct ratios. Amidst this advanced equipment was an ancient carbon-arc slide projector, still used for advertisements, which could also be adapted for use as a spotlight. The projection room, spacious by the standards of most small cinemas, was under the control of chief projectionist Peter Delnevo, who had started at the Scala aged fifteen and worked there for twenty-five years until 1970.

It was a big shock for the long-serving staff to learn that the family-run cinema had been sold to Star Associated Holdings of Leeds in June 1970. Eric Bowtell said that the sale was not because the Scala was run down, but because he wanted to do things he had not had the chance to do with the problems of a business hanging over him.

Star immediately set about changing the style and pace at the Scala. Sunday opening was introduced immediately. Plans were soon drawn up for conversion to a twin cinema and the Scala closed its doors on Saturday 24 October after a showing of *Spartacus*. The builders moved in the day after and by the Monday afternoon, seating and projection equipment was being removed. The auditorium was divided across the middle and two small cinemas built one behind

Star publicity shows the ingenious creation of two cinemas within the old Scala to form Studios 1 and 2 in 1970. (CTA)

The Phoenix, Walton Street in 2005. (IM)

the other. Studio 2 – the smaller, seating 141 – was built in the back stalls and Studio 1 (250 seats) was at the front, with the screen in the original position. The old projection room was kept, using a periscope system to project down into Studio 2 and direct projection to Studio 1, the beam passing between the original roof and the rafters of the new Studio 2. Four Westar projectors with BTH xenon lamphouses were installed. Both auditoria had screens without front tabs, Studio 1 having a floating screen backed by gold curtains. Both cinemas were luxuriously carpeted and fitted with new seating. The façade was modernised and the foyer narrowed, with a concessions stand included. Three large cubes emblazoned with '1 & 2' were fitted on the front of the cinema and film titles were displayed on a new backlit triangular canopy.

Studios 1 and 2 opened on 28 December 1970 with Richard Burton and Genevieve Bujold in *Anne of the Thousand Days* and Kirk Douglas in *There Was a Crooked Man*. However, programming soon degenerated, with Studio 2 becoming Studio X private cinema club on 11 July 1976, featuring uncensored films rather different to the *Virtuous Wives* shown at the 1920 gala evening. The first programme for club members was *Animal Love* and *Ramrodder* – enough said. The cinema was taken over by Contemporary Films and renamed the Phoenix on 17 July 1977, reverting to art-house programming on both screens; it narrowly escaped sale to Cannon Cinemas in 1985 when, following a public campaign, manager Bob Orde and Tony Jones of the Cambridge Arts Cinema combined to put the cinema on a firm footing and introduced a Friends of the Phoenix scheme. In 1992 it was taken over by a small company, City Screen, which has since grown to be a major exhibitor with stylish cinemas across the country, including locally at Henley-on-Thames. They have kept the cinema up to date both technically and in patron comfort, adding an attractive café-bar in an unused area between the front wall and the projection room and improving the frontage. Projection is now by two Westar projectors with tower system and from February 2007 the Phoenix was also equipped in both screens for digital projection as well as film. The periscope system in Screen 2 has been replaced by more satisfactory direct projection and the false ceiling has been removed from Screen 1 to reveal the attractive ceiling trough lighting. Current seating is for 201 and 98.

The New Cinema/Headington Cinema/Moulin Rouge/Not the Moulin Rouge

Another small venue with a chequered history, the cinema now best remembered as the Moulin Rouge was the enterprise of Edwin (James) Hall whose varied career had included employment as a shipping clerk and a period in Canada where he ran a number of shops. When he returned to England he moved to 24 London Road, Headington (latterly number 9) where he built three shops onto the front of his house and a cinema in the garden.

The New Cinema, built by Kingerlee and believed to have been designed by architect J.C. Leed of Cornmarket, Oxford, was entered from New High Street, with the auditorium at right angles behind other buildings. The 500 seats were all on one floor and the projection room was up wooden stairs reached from the garden through a door in the gents. The New Cinema celebrated its opening on 5 October 1923 with the first of the two feature-length parts of the Frits Lang film *Dr Mabuse, der Spieler (Dr Mabuse the Gambler)*. Being silent, 'foreign' films were, of course, universal, with only the intertitles needing changing to the appropriate language. Supporting this epic were *Lilac Sunbonnet*, a serial and a documentary. The grand opening lived up to its advertising with the 'largest programme on record.' The second chapter of the story of arch-criminal *Dr Mabuse* was shown on Thursday to Saturday of the first week, supported by the drama *Solomon in Society*. Matinees were held on Thursday and Saturday, doors opening on other days at 5.30 p.m. Seats were reservable and music was from an orchestra directed by Mr H.C. Stewart.

Sound was introduced in 1930, using sound-on-disc, which was replaced in 1933 with the sound-on-film system. For two years from 1930, the cinema was leased to a London concern, Commercial and Maritime Film Service of Denmark Street, but James Hall took it back and, with his son Edward, ran the Headington Cinema (the 'new' was dropped around 1929) until his death on 1 January 1960. Edward Hall leased the cinema to Unifilms of Wardour Street, who gave it a general facelift; now renamed the Ciné Moulin Rouge it reopened on 23 January 1961 with a special presentation of *Black Orpheus*, the 1960 Academy Award winner for the category of best foreign film. Oxford City Council planners had refused Unifilms' application to put up an illuminated windmill sign with revolving sails, but when the mayor and mayoress turned up for the grand opening they were greeted by a gendarme and can-can dancers (shades of things

The New Cinema, New High Street, Headington, 1920s. (Jeremy's of Oxford)

to come). The latter were described as models from Elliston's, the department store – whether live or mannequins is not clear from the report.

However, the stability of being run as a family business had been lost, and a series of proprietors, openings and closings followed rapidly: Bill Maelor-Jones in 1962, followed by Stephen Wischhusen's company Provincial Electric Theatres. In 1977 the cinema closed on 27 August with *Benji* and *The Seven Voyages of Sinbad*, only to reopen on 12 September with *California Split* and *Bite the Bullet*. Programming moved towards 'sexploitation' movies, an unsuitable choice for a cinema in a family residential area. On 15 July 1978 there was a further closure with *Sex Sisters* and *Girls for Rent* following a loss of a Kinematograph Renters' Society allocation of product hearing against EMI/ABC, which if successful would have given the Moulin Rouge a better access to new mainstream films.

On 6 August Graham Steane-Byers (Mayfair Films) took over. The troubles continued, and on 20 March 1980 the Official Receiver stepped in to close the cinema before the showing of *Daughter of Emanuelle* and *Mondo Erotica*. This really did seem to be the end, but rescue came in the form of Bill Heine, proprietor of the Penultimate Picture Palace who lived near to the closed cinema. He reopened it on 1 November, at a stroke lifting the quality of programming with Roman Polanski's *Tess*.

When he reopened the cinema, Bill Heine put up a sculpture of a pair of high-kicking can-can legs on the top of the frontage. The planners, predictably, objected, arguing that the 15ft sculpture was an advertisement, required planning permission, and advised against granting it. They should have known better. Bill Heine argued that they were a work of art and therefore not covered by planning laws. To underline his point, he changed the name of the cinema to

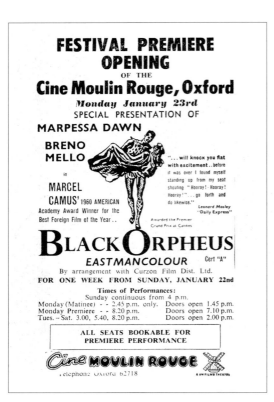

The Headington Cinema opens as the Cine Moulin Rouge in 1961. (Giles Woodforde)

The Headington as the Moulin Rouge in the 1970s. (CTA)

Final curtain – the demolition of the *Not the Moulin Rouge* in 1991. (IM)

Not the Moulin Rouge, to demonstrate that the legs were clearly *not* an advertisement for the Moulin Rouge! In the event, councillors voted to let the legs stay, rejecting the recommendation of their planning officer, and they remained, brightening up the street, attracting tourists and even appearing on a postcard.

On 12 May 1991, what proved to be the last show was presented, Jean Renoir's 1939 *La Règle du Jeu* (The Rules of the Game). Staff arrived the next day and found the doors padlocked against them. The cinema was demolished soon after and has now been replaced by housing. Seating on closure was 350, having reached a high of 600 in 1941. Projection equipment since around 1948 had been Ross projectors with Peerless arcs, changed towards the end to Westar projectors.

But there is a postscript. The sculpture of the legs was removed to Bill Heine's cinema in Brighton, the historic Duke of York's. By a happy coincidence, the planning officer who had recommended their removal in Oxford had by this time become the Borough Planning Officer in – you've guessed it, Brighton. Mr Heine said, 'He lost round one of the battle. If there is to be a round two, he would do well to remember that they deliver a hefty kick and ought to be treated to the respect due to a heavyweight.' They still kick out over the frontage of the cinema in Brighton.

The Oxford/Oxford Super Cinema/Super/ABC/MGM/Cannon/ABC/Odeon Magdalen Street
The next cinema development was back in the city centre, for the Oxford Cinematograph Theatre Co. (1922) Ltd, the proprietors of the nearby George Street Cinema. Built on the site of

Collins' carriage factory, this was to be a much more opulent affair, 'super' in name and nature. The architects were Frank Matcham & Co. of London and J.C. Leed of Oxford. Matcham himself had been a noted theatre architect, but by the time the Super was built he had retired and died, the firm now being under the control of his former chief assistant Francis Graham Moon Chancellor. The main contractors were Hinkins & Frewin of Oxford.

The main entrance was of marble surrounded by a bronze, illuminated fascia. A long vestibule led to a spacious lounge, treated in rich French Renaissance style with mirrors. There was a tearoom above. The auditorium, with stalls and balcony, was richly decorated, each wall bearing a large 30ft-long by 17ft-high painting, one depicting 'Modern Sport' and the other 'Modern Learning'; these were painted by G. Rushton, R.B.A. Each side of the proscenium were decorative grilles and large urns stood in niches in the side walls beside the paintings. There was seating for 1,300, 950 in the stalls and 350 in the balcony. The small fireproof projection room was built very high up on the roof outside the main body of the cinema.

The Oxford opened on 1 January 1924; Lord Valentia gave a speech (he was getting used to this, having opened the George Street Cinema) and pronounced that 'the cinema was here to stay'. The first night film was *Armageddon*, with *The Four Horsemen of the Apocalypse* showing for the rest of the week. An orchestra directed by William Childs provided the all-important music. A two-manual Spurden Rutt 'Organestra' organ was installed in 1928, one of the only three of this make ever installed in cinemas. The first public performance was at a Grand Organ Recital in aid of charity given by Stanley Hemery A.R.C.O. on 21 October, supported by other musicians, and supplemented by films about Schubert and Mendelssohn.

The Oxford Super Cinema, as it advertised itself, was the first in Oxford to install sound, opening with *Broadway Melody* on 6 January 1930. The rest of the programme consisted of silent films, accompanied by orchestra and organ, but their days were numbered. The new installation was clearly not satisfactory as, following a showing of Al Jolson in *The Singing Fool* on 29 March, the Super reverted to silent films for a week whilst the sound equipment was replaced with Western Electric. The old projectors were removed and the new ones installed on concrete bases overnight midweek, without missing a performance. In 1932 it was taken over by Union Cinemas.

During 1935 the stage was extended over the orchestra pit, the orchestra having been dispensed with. The organ was now entombed below the stage and not 'rediscovered' until a group of enthusiasts uncovered it around 1965. It has since been removed and rebuilt, its present home being at Rounce Farm Barn in Woking, Surrey, where it can now be played after suffering nearly seventy years of silence.

The most dramatic changes came with the ABC makeover in the 1970s when the foyer mirrors were covered over and the decorative elements in the auditorium covered by curtaining. A much more sympathetic treatment was given in 2001, especially in the auditorium, where features have now been delicately picked out, although curtaining still covers the paintings and vases, which still remain. One problem since the introduction of Cinemascope has been the limitation of the proscenium frame. Complaints that the picture is too small have resulted in the top masking actually being lowered to get the correct ratio for scope so that the picture is actually smaller. However, the Odeon Magdalen Street, as it is now known, is the only place in Oxford where the feeling of seeing a film in a 'super' cinema of the past can still be recaptured. With 647 seats, it is exactly half its original capacity, the balcony in particular having been reduced in capacity to give greater comfort. The building is Grade II listed.

Odeon created a small second screen in the former café which had long gone. The original plasterwork can still be seen but even by modern standards this sixty-one-seater is too small to give a 'big screen' experience and of Odeon's eight screens in Oxford this is the least successful.

Right and below: The Oxford Super Cinema,
Magdalen Street, in the 1930s. (CTA)

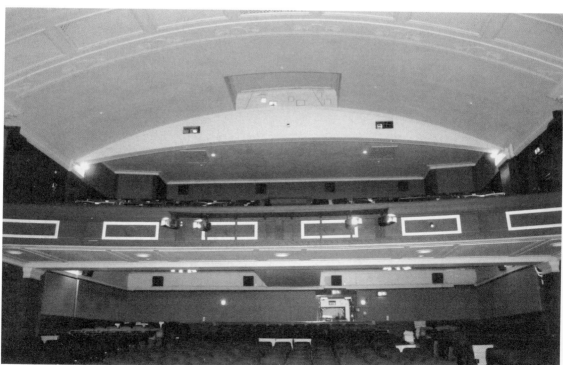

This page: The former restaurant of the Oxford Super was stripped (Geoff Chandler) and fitted out as the tiny Odeon Screen 2 in Magdalen Street. (IM)

Opposite, above and below: The main architectural features of the Super remain in today's Odeon, Magdalen Street. (IM)

The Rink/Majestic Cinema

One of the shortest-lived cinemas in the county, the Majestic in Botley Road saw more drama off the screen than on it during its few years of operation.

This hangar-like building, with white show frontage, was designed by architect John R. Wilkins who had already produced two of Oxford's early cinemas, the Electric in Castle Street and the Picture Palace in Jeune Street. It originally opened on 7 November 1930 as Oxford Ice Skating Rink; in 1933 it was temporarily converted for the summer season to The Rink Cinema, opening with 1,500 seats for a pre-release première of the musical *The Viennese Waltz*, supported by comedies and the latest newsreel. The opening ceremony on 24 July was performed by the mayor, Alderman C.H. Brown, clearly delighted to appear 'behind the footlights' as he put it.

Claiming to be Oxford's largest picture theatre, The Rink boasted generous spacing between seats, no queues, moderate prices (4d to 1s 10d) and a large restaurant. It was an instant success and was filled each evening of the opening week with appreciative audiences. The opening coincided with a heatwave, the *Oxford Times* reporting that The Rink was 'one of the coolest places to go'. Welcome during hot weather, this coolness was to prove one of the less popular features in cold spells and, indeed, apart from the unusually wide spacing between rows, this was the aspect best recalled by patrons who remember going there.

The screen was 'one of the largest and finest in the country' and anticipated acoustic problems with the BT-H sound system did not materialise. The shallow balcony, designed for viewing the skating, was particularly praised for its spacious comfort.

The Rink's cinema season closed on 7 October 1933 with a comedy programme that included Laurel and Hardy in *Beau Chumps*. As planned, it reverted to ice skating for the winter season from 14 October 1933 to 9 March 1934. The proprietors were obviously pleased with their venture into films, however; the rink re-opened as the Majestic Cinema on Easter Monday, 2 April with increased seating of 1,900. This time the changes were permanent; a new raked floor had been put down, and the viewing gallery had been replaced by a more conventional (although rather shallow) cinema balcony. Some of the seats had come from the 'old' New Theatre in George Street which had recently been demolished to make way for the present-day theatre.

This time the launch did not go quite so smoothly. The advertised civic opening by the mayor Alderman Miss Tawney was abandoned because of the controversial choice of film, *I'm No Angel*, starring Mae West. The mayor felt unable to associate her office with a film publicised as being about 'a sensitive gal who climbed the ladder of success … wrong by wrong!'.

Luckily, the Oxford public did not share Miss Tawney's finer feelings and turned out in droves. On the first day 5,000 attended and the police had to be called in to control the queues and traffic. Manager Mr A.P. Iliffe read cablegrams of good wishes from Mae West herself as well as from stars Marlene Dietrich, Carole Lombard, Gary Cooper and George Raft.

Ownership was variously by Oxford Ice Skating Rink Ltd, Majestic Cinema (Oxford) Ltd and Reeds Theatres Ltd of 104-08 Oxford Street, London. The cinema was managed on behalf of the owners by Union Cinemas (and later by ABC together with the other Union houses) with prices from 5d to 2s 4d. The venue also boasted a café and dance hall, the latter used for the Oxford Cinemas' Social Club dance.

War intervened, and the cinema closed suddenly on 11 September 1940 in the middle of the run of *Babes in Arms*, starring Mickey Rooney and Judy Garland. Large numbers of unofficial evacuees had arrived in Oxford from London and the building was taken over as an emergency depot to house them. Up to 5,000 passed through the building, and instead of the advertised programme 5 tons of straw had to be purchased by the Evacuation Officer to fill mattresses.

This page: The Oxford Skating Rink (interior photograph of rink OCCPA) became the Rink/Majestic Cinema on a permanent basis in 1934. (Photographs of cinema: CTA)

The celebrated wide row spacing came into its own. The grassed area outside soon became litter strewn and Vera Brittain, visiting Oxford, gives a graphic description in *England's Hour* of what she found inside:

> As I enter the cinema, a familiar and overpowering stench strikes me on the face like a blow … Covering the floor between the upturned velveteen seats of the cinema chairs, disorderly piles of mattresses, pillows, rugs and cushions indicate the 'pitches' staked out by the different evacuated families. Many of the women, too dispirited to move, still lie wearily on the floor with their children beside them in the fetid air, though the hour is 11 a.m. and a warm sun is shining cheerfully on the city streets. Between the mattresses and cushions, the customary collection of soiled newspapers and ancient apple cores is contributing noticeably to the odoriferous atmosphere. A few small boys, evidently set to the task by the organisers on the floor above, are making a determined attack on the extensive squalor with besoms and brooms.

The situation led to questions in the House of Commons and, although the building was closed to evacuees in January 1941, the screen was to remain dark forever. Immediately after the evacuees had arrived in 1940, press advertisements had indicated that this closure was only temporary, and that announcements would be made on all ABC screens about the Majestic's reopening. Whether this was really the intention at the time, or whether ABC was glad of the opportunity to rid itself of one of a number of white elephants inherited in the Union legacy, is not known.

Over time the building served as a hostel for local employer Pressed Steel, a Frank Cooper marmalade factory and finally an MFI showroom, losing all internal features and the balcony from its brief cinema days; skylight panels had been inserted in the curved roof. The outside remained substantially unchanged from its original Ice Rink days although the added projection room over the entrance was a giveaway to cinema spotters.

Many people browsed amongst the bedroom and kitchen displays over the years without any idea of the chequered history of this unique building. It was finally demolished in the 1980s and replaced with purpose-built retail buildings housing MFI and Halfords.

The Playhouse Theatres

The original Playhouse started life in 1923 in a barn-like building in Woodstock Road which had been a big game museum exhibiting stuffed animals. It had closed in December 1929 and was being used as a midget golf-course when in July 1930 an advertisement in the *Oxford Times* announced the Grand Public Opening of the Oxford Playhouse as a Cinema and Variety Hall. The mayor was to officiate, and a 'first-class variety company' was promised. This event never took place, the theatre instead reopening with a season of plays presented by Sir Philip Ben Greet. The old building was renamed the Red Barn Theatre after the new Oxford Playhouse opened.

The current Oxford Playhouse opened in 1938 in Beaumont Street; it was fitted with 35mm projection equipment in 1990 by City Screen who ran the Phoenix Cinema in Walton Street. According to a press release, the idea was to present a series of 'Oscars in Oxford' and special one-off premieres. In the event, only a handful of films were ever shown and the theatre is no longer equipped for film. It had been rumoured during the 1960s that Odeon (Rank) were considering it as a possible cinema, but luckily that came to nothing and the Playhouse continues as a comfortable and intimate venue to enjoy live theatre.

Ritz/ABC/MGM/Cannon/ABC/Odeon George Street

Union Cinemas opened the Ritz in Gloucester Green in 1936 as a replacement for the demolished George Street Cinema. The neighbouring St George's church was also pulled down

The present Oxford Playhouse in Beaumont Street, used for the occasional film presentation in the early 1990s. (IM)

to make room for the auditorium. Seating 1,654 patrons, it was the flagship of the Union circuit's growing Oxford interests and was built in seven months in a 'transitional modern treatment' to the designs of their chief architect, Robert Cromie. The main entrance faced a new street constructed at right angles to George Street, and featured large windows (opening onto the café on one floor and the manager's office above) over a canopy. A low relief by sculptor Newbury Trent was located immediately above the central window. In order to maximise seating, the plain brick auditorium was built parallel to George Street on the one side and Gloucester Green on the other, the use of special narrower bricks emphasising its mass.

The interior decoration was in beige, pink and gold. The proscenium was framed by a lighting cove with a grille for the organ chambers in the centre above. There was a three-manual, six-unit Compton organ with Melotone electronic unit, with a 'phantom piano' on stage, played from the console that rose on a lift from the centre of the orchestra pit. Full stage facilities were provided and projection was by Kalee projectors with Western Electric Wide Range sound reproduction.

The opening charity performance on 20 April 1936 (25 per cent going to the Cinematograph Trade Benevolent Fund and 75 per cent to the Radcliffe Infirmary) was a major civic occasion. The formal opening was by the mayor, Alderman Mrs M.G. Townsend, and the audience included the Duke and Duchess of Marlborough, together with film stars Margaret Lockwood and John Stuart. Gaumont-British cameramen were present to record the events for showing later in the week.

Above and below: The Ritz, George Street, was Oxford's most prestigious venue. (CTA)

The programme included a fanfare and the national anthem by the Bach Trumpeters of the Royal Military School of Music and a recital by Alex Taylor on the Compton organ. The main feature was *The Guv'nor* (George Arliss), supported by a Disney *Silly Symphony* cartoon *Three Orphan Kittens* and a newsreel. The spectacular stage show featured The Seven Graysons (a springboard and balancing act), dancing by the Ten Gordon Ray Girls, Van Dock (the Royal Command Performance lightning cartoon artist), and Macari and his Dutch Accordion Serenaders.

The Ritz passed to ABC and continued as the premier Oxford cinema, a status underlined when it was the first in Oxford to be converted for cinemascope and later, in 1959, for the new large screen process Todd-AO, at a cost of £25,000. The installation included the new giant screen (50ft by 24ft) set in front of the proscenium arch and the construction of a new projection room at the back of the circle to give a more level throw. This new arrangement put the stage permanently out of use. Sound and vision were spectacular, with 70mm film and six magnetic soundtracks fed into five stage and eighteen auditorium speakers. The two projectors were state of the art Philips DP70 with Mole-Richardson carbon arcs and were capable of handling regular 35mm widescreen and scope films, for which the black masking closed down to give a smaller screen size. The arcs were later replaced by Peerless Magnarcs which were cheaper to run.

The first 70mm presentation was *South Pacific* on 22 February 1959. Separate performances were given at roadshow prices, and in the evenings Albert Brierley entertained on the Compton organ. The film was still running in London at the Dominion, Tottenham Court Road, after eleven months.

At the beginning of March 1963 the name Ritz was dropped in favour of plain ABC, in line with circuit policy to strengthen the brand. A few days later, on Tuesday 12 March, a police constable on night patrol saw smoke coming from the cinema and raised the alarm at 2.40 a.m. By the time the fire brigade broke in, there was a fire raging upstairs, in the stalls and on the stage. To add insult to injury for the fire fighters, at one point it was feared that the fire might spread to the fire station, which adjoined the stage end of the building.

Projectionist John Sharp was woken up by his mother who had been told there had been a fire at the Ritz. He went down to work and everyone on the bus was talking about it. He assumed little damage would have been done, but reality was different:

> When we went in, it was awful. All you could see was the screen frame and pieces of tabs hanging. Luckily, the projection room was not touched, except everything was black from the smoke, even though the fire had started under the circle, probably caused by a cigarette.

Graham Wintle, then chief projectionist at the Regal and later chief at the ABC George Street itself, also remembers coming down and 'everything was black'. The projection room had escaped because the fire shutters behind the glass ports were regularly closed down at night. Originally designed to protect the audience from fires in the box, this time they had worked in reverse and saved the box from a fire in the auditorium. The rear stalls were completely destroyed as was the £600 screen.

The manager (Albert T. 'Jack' Frost), having been called from his bed, had already put up a sign to say that the cinema would reopen as soon as possible. This did not actually happen until October. The projection team stayed there for two weeks, cleaning up the projection room and then two of them went up to the Regal, Cowley Road for six months until reopening – a generous gesture by ABC. Chief projectionist Jock Anderson and the trainee stayed at George Street. The film at the time of the fire was Judy Garland in *I Could Go On Singing*. How wrong she was that week.

The coming of Todd-AO: roadshow presentations commence with *South Pacific* in 1959. (Giles Woodforde)

Rather than repair, the auditorium was completely remodelled, with sweeping golden tabs and drapes stretching from one side of the circle to the other, bigger and more comfortable seats (with more legroom in the stalls – reducing seating by a further 212) and an ornate fibrous plaster ceiling by G.J. Green & Sons of London. New air conditioning was installed and the theatre was completely rewired. The organ survived, but sustained damage. Although the original intention was to restore it, in the event it was sold back to the John Compton company for spares. The reconstruction project was led by Don Berry and Jack Sutton of ABC's in-house architects' team. The longest 'road-show' presentation was *The Sound of Music* which opened on Boxing Day 1965 'for a season'. The season turned out to be fifty-eight weeks and the film was shown 810 times before ending on 4 February 1967 to make way for *My Fair Lady*.

In 1975 the cinema was tripled, the circle being extended forward as ABC 1 and the stalls being divided into two smaller cinemas, side by side. The DP70 equipment, considered the Rolls-Royce of the projector world, was removed and abandoned on the old stage area and subsequently, it is believed, sold to Japan. ABC publicity described the décor and seating as:

Screen 1: Deep purple ceiling, with mauve walls, red seating and carpets (612 seats)
Screen 2: Tones of French blue with Royal blue ceiling (322 seats)
Screen 3: Shades of wine and plum with red seating and carpet (141 seats)
.

The cinemas opened towards the end of 1975: ABC 1 on 16 November with *Black Christmas* and *Out of Service*; ABC 2 on 14 December with *Barry Lyndon*; and ABC 3 on the same day with *Inside Out* and *The Deadly Trap*.

Reconstruction of the ABC Oxford, after the 1963 fire, resulted in an impressive sweep of curtaining and modern styling. (Newsquest)

The next change came in 2001, when further subdivision into six screens took place and the cinema adopted the Odeon name and house style. Screen 1 (the old circle) has been split into two 252-seat screens, now numbered 1 and 2; Screen 3 was built in a new space over the entrance foyer created by knocking out the floor between the old café and the manager's office above and seats 111; Screens 4 and 5 were the previous stalls cinemas 2 and 3 and seat 140 and 239 respectively; and Screen 6, seating 129, is located in the former stage area. All six are fitted with Kineton projectors with platters, spread between four projection rooms. The one projection team operates both the Odeons, George Street and nearby Magdalen Street, giving them six projection rooms and eight screens spread between two buildings.

This is the current state of play. However, in 2005 it was announced that AXA Sun Life had put forward plans to demolish the Odeon, George Street and replace it with shops and restaurants, with cinemas on upper floors. This plan is supported by Oxford City Council, the owner of the freehold; the lease expires in 2009.

Regal

The Regal was the last of Oxford's super cinemas to be built and was situated on the corner of Cowley Road and Magdalen Road (not to be confused with Magdalen *Street*). It was opened on 9 April 1937 by Union Cinemas, twelve months after the Ritz, and was Union's sixth cinema in Oxford; by this point the circuit had nearly 250 cinemas overall. Designed by the same architect, Robert Cromie, and with 1,674 seats, it had great similarities to its elder sibling, although people who remember both in their heyday often express a preference for the Regal. The main contractor was Marfix & Co. Ltd.

Above and below: Odeon, George Street, Oxford: removal of the floor between the old restaurant and the manager's office, and widening of the upstairs projection room in order to create more screens in 2001. (Geoff Chandler)

Above and below: The new Screens 1 and 3 in the Odeon, George Street. (IM)

An immediately striking feature was the 24ft-high entry foyer, with decorative mirrors, water fountain, chandeliers and painted ceiling panels. Full stage facilities were again provided, and there was a Compton organ with three manuals and five units. Seating was in soft, salmon-coloured velvet with padded arms and wider than average row spacing. Ante-proscenium grilles of intricate design were picked out in shades of red and gold, but these did not hide the organ pipes, which were situated under the stage – a big mistake, as we shall see. The projection room (too big to be called a box!) was equipped with two Kalee projectors and Western Electric Mirrophonic sound, recently developed and claiming 'a new beauty of sound, clarity and illusion of reality reproduced'. Also provided were two spotlights and a slide projector.

The opening night was a typically grand Union affair. The ceremony was performed by Oxford's deputy-mayor, Councillor Mrs Mary Townsend, who had also opened the Ritz. Stage attractions included Zigano's Anglo French Accordion Band, Stanford and McNaughton the wise jesters, the Three Lorandos (comedy acrobats on a wire), the Eight Dancing Daughters plus BBC and recording star Sidney Torch at the mighty Compton organ. The opening film was *O.H.M.S.* starring Wallace Ford.

The Regal was set in a residential area and attracted large audiences from the start. It passed to the control of ABC in October 1937 and carried on as a highly successful venture. The location of the organ under the stage had caused problems, however, as the Regal was prone to understage flooding – a problem that persists to the present day. It was removed to the Ritz, Keighley within the first year of operation.

As time progressed, the Regal, like all cinemas, was suffering from dwindling audiences, primarily because of television. ABC introduced bingo for two nights a week, with films on five nights from Saturday to Wednesday. Bingo was an instant success, and it was inevitable that the Regal should go over to the game on a full-time basis. The last programme, *The Haunted House of Horrors* and *Clegg*, was shown on Wednesday 1 July 1970. The closing choice of films (horror and a 'private eye thriller in which a series of murders is punctuated with nudity sequences', *Oxford Times*) rather sums up the Regal as the poor relation to the two city-centre ABC houses. It reopened as an ABC Social Club from Saturday 4 July; it was run for a period by the Star Group, taken back by EMI Social Centres Ltd in 1975, and finally operated by Gala Bingo. On 3 August 2004 it was Grade II listed.

When Gala moved out to a new site on the Ozone Leisure Park (next to the Vue Cinema) and the building stood empty and for sale, the listed status undoubtedly saved it from mutilation or destruction. Enter local business owner Younis Ali, who had always felt a close affinity for the Regal. He had attended the ABC Minors and at a young age sold newspapers outside. The people in the queues used to be very friendly to him, especially the bingo ladies – he remembers the massive queues when the game was initially introduced for two nights. When the Regal came up for sale he had no hesitation in buying it. He hopes it can be used for concerts, meetings, parties and hopefully some films in the future.

Meanwhile, Gala had left the building with a floor levelled out to stage height, but with the cinema seating still in place in the circle. Much of the original decorative work, including the grilles, is still in place. It is paradoxical that the Regal, in common with a number of our remaining 'super' cinema buildings throughout the country, has survived intact without subdivision only because of the very game which hastened its downfall.

The main features of the beautiful foyer are still present, but hidden at the lower levels by subsequently added sales structures and extra doors for fire precautions. Much of this clutter is reversible, however. Up in the projection room, two Ross model 3 projectors with Peerless arcs and Western Electric sound remain (but without their motors and lenses). There are also two spotlights and a bi-unial (double-lensed) slide lantern, all heavily decorated by pigeons over thirty-six years since they were last used. Restoration is in progress.

Above and below: Union's second 'super cinema', the Regal, Cowley Road, opened in 1937. Like the Ritz, the architect was Robert Cromie.

Left, below and opposite: Much of the original decoration and equipment (such as this stage lighting board) survives in the Regal, Cowley Road, as these 2006 pictures show. (IM)

Ozone/Vue

After much delay and wrangling, Oxford (and Oxfordshire) finally got its first multiplex in 2003. Of a number of plans and sites that had come and gone over the years, it was the Minchery Farm proposal put forward by Oxford United Football Club chairman Firoz Kassam that finally won through.

The opening of the Ozone multiplex in Grenoble Road was not without controversy. Oxford United had been given the green light to build a new stadium, funded by the Ozone Leisure Park, which was to include a bowl, fitness centre, dance studio, bingo, restaurants, a hotel and the cinema. Opposition came from many quarters, including the local brewer, residents concerned about a late licence, South Oxfordshire District Council (which favoured a Didcot location for a multiplex), ABC, which had an alternative plan, a developer which had been turned down for a twelve-screen cinema in Oxpens Road, and sundry parish councils. A public enquiry was considered and there was a threat of a judicial review. In 1999 John Prescott, then Environment Secretary, decided not to intervene and the City Council granted planning permission.

Even then, it was not plain sailing for the new cinema. The planning permission restricted cinema opening on match days at the adjacent stadium, and Vue, the prospective operator, withdrew. Firoz Kassam decided to run the cinema himself until the planning issues could be resolved, and the £8 million Ozone nine-screen multiplex opened on 16 December 2003, all seats being £1 on the first night. Opening films included *Finding Nemo*, *Down with Love*, *Calendar Girls*, *American Pie – the Wedding* and *Intolerable Cruelty*. *Lord of the Rings – Return of the King* opened the next day. A Saturday morning show called Movie Mob was introduced and a Senior Screen on Wednesday mornings.

Above and below: Cinema-going for the twenty-first century: The Vue Multiplex in Oxford with its spacious projection room in 2007. (IM)

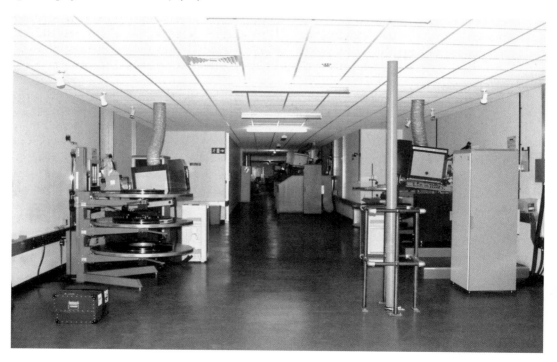

The complex seats 2,000 people in nine auditoria numbered 1, 5, and 6–12. Provision has been made for the screens 2–4 but these are shells and have not been fitted out. Projection is by Italian Cinemeccanica equipment with Christie platters and Dolby sound, all in one long projection room. Screens run wall-to-wall, giving a very large picture; all auditoria are stepped, with excellent sightlines and comfortable seats.

Despite dire predictions, Kassam showed that an independent could book films and make a success of a multiplex. As he had claimed, it was 'not rocket science'. The Ozone continued to show films when the stadium was in use despite the planning restriction, and this was eventually lifted. In 2005 the multiplex transferred to Vue as a going concern and the cinema was advertised under its new name from 4 November.

SHIPTON-UNDER-WYCHWOOD

In 1941 Dr Gordon Scott, a local GP, proposed a forward-looking scheme for the conversion of a disused building, St Michael's House, into a centre which would include a school, doctor's surgery and leisure facilities including swimming pool, library, tennis courts and a cinema-cum-theatre. Although £2,500 was raised towards the required £3,000, the ambitious scheme was unfortunately abandoned in 1946. During the war Dr Scott had arranged for films to be shown in the village hall by the Revd Thomas Wood of Charlbury. Shortly after, the village was to get its own proper cinema.

Wychwood Cinema

The Wychwood in Upper High Street started life in a plain flat-roofed building next to The Lamb shortly after the war. During the war, Alf Bayliss had used it as a factory for making wooden cases for gramophones and cash registers (hence the location being known as the Till Yard). The cinema was set up and operated by A.J. 'Nobby' Clarke, who also ran a shop in the village. It was fitted out with tip-up seats for around 100 people. Roy Marshall remembers that there was originally only one projector so there were breaks for reel changes every twenty minutes; later a second projector was added, but either the aperture plates or lenses were not matched properly as the picture changed size when reel changeovers were made.

Initially, the Wychwood advertised very briefly in the *Oxford Times*, the first being for the week of 13 May 1946, when the main feature was Wilfrid Lawson and Ann Todd in *Danny Boy*. This may have been the actual opening programme but if not it was certainly very early in the life of the cinema. Two programmes were shown each week – Monday to Wednesday and Thursday to Saturday, with one show nightly at 7.30 p.m. The 'full supporting programme' included *Paramount News*.

Local people remember that going to the Wychwood was not always a comfortable experience. In addition to projection problems, the auditorium always seemed cold; even the plush tip-up seats could be a hazard as it was advisable before sitting down to check that one of Mr Clarke's free-ranging hens hadn't laid an egg in the hollow of the seat! In 1950, at Chadlington petty sessions the magistrates adjourned for two weeks an application from Mr Clarke for the granting of a theatre licence, but gave provisional approval for the renewal of his cinema licence. Police Superintendent Harris reported that, 'some of the wiring was crude, and that there was a large combustion stove which was a fire risk'. Mr Clarke assured the magistrates that the wiring had been attended to and that if a licence were granted for a stage he would get a central heating plant. Unfortunately there is no report of the final outcome of this application.

WYCHWOOD CINEMA
SHIPTON-UNDER-WYCHWOOD

Mon., Tues., Wed. Next, at 7.30
FRANK RANDLE
in
"HOME SWEET HOME"
With RAWICZ and LANDAUER, the
World Famous Duo-Pianists
And SUPPORTING PROGRAMME

Thurs., Fri., Sat. Next, at 7.30
JAMES CAGNEY   PAT O'BRIEN
in
"THE IRISH IN US"
And SUPPORTING PROGRAMME
Prices 1 0. 1/- Children 10d.

WYCHWOOD CINEMA
SHIPTON-UNDER-WYCHWOOD

Mon., Tues., Wed. Next, at 7.30
BETTE DAVIS, PAUL LUKAS
in
"WATCH on the RHINE"
And SUPPORTING PROGRAMME

Thurs., Fri., Sat. Next, at 7.30
Ida Lupino - Dennis Morgan
in
"THE HARD WAY"
And SUPPORTING PROGRAMME

Wychwood Cinema programmes for May 1946.

The Wychwood stopped its newspaper advertising after a few weeks and was never listed as a venue in the *Kine Year Book*. After it closed (probably in the late 1950s) the building was used by a Mr Newbold for storing pig feed. Films were shown in the old village hall after the cinema had closed down.

SHRIVENHAM

See Services cinemas

THAME

(Provincial) Electric Picture Palace / Thame Picture Palace (Chinnor Road)
'Notice! Notice! To the inhabitants of Thame and District', cried the advertisement in the *Thame Gazette* announcing the opening of the Provincial Electric Picture Palace in 1913. The Town Hall had been used as a film venue for visiting shows before Thame got its first proper cinema, which was opened by Mr B.W. Liddington JP on the afternoon of Thursday 12 June. He was very complimentary to the proprietors and hoped they would receive ample reward for the money they had invested. Unfortunately this opening show (which was in aid of the Nursing Home) was not as well supported as could have been desired. 'Various excellent pictures were thrown on the sheet and much enjoyed whilst the Misses Wells and Walker played a duet and Mrs Brazell sang a song'. The 'various excellent pictures' included the dramas *The Making of Broncho Billy* and *Dr Maxwell's Experiment* together with a number of 'very laughable pieces' including

A Pair of Braces and *After the Welsh Rabbit*. The Picture Palace ('Provincial' was dropped after the first week) opened to better audiences for the rest of the week, including a special matinee for 407 school children on the Friday.

The proprietors of the enterprise were builder R.G. Holland of 21 Park Street, who acted as resident manager, and C. Lester, the ironmonger of Upper High Street. Prices ran from 3d up to 1s. The Picture Palace opened on Monday and Tuesday, then from Thursday to Saturday. There was one show nightly and a special matinee for children on Saturday afternoons. The building was on a plot on the corner of Chinnor Road (wrongly advertised as Park Street in the original advertisement) and Croft Road, in front of the Globe Iron Works and immediately opposite the police station. From the Ordnance Survey map of 1921, the auditorium ran parallel to Chinnor Road. Seating was for 300 and piano music was provided, one of the earliest pianists being a teenager named Doris West.

Thame Picture Palace closed after the last performance of *The Face at the Window* on Saturday 26 November 1921 until the new cinema was opened. Unusually in such circumstances, there was a gap of nine months between the closing of the old and the opening of the new, which was filled by visits of Purchase's Electric Biograph to the Town Hall. The old Picture Palace was used for some kind of industrial purpose and eventually demolished; the site is now occupied by Croft Court, flats built in 1965 by the Thame and District Housing Association. The building seems to follow the same footprint, giving a good idea of the size of this small edge-of-town picture house.

An aerial view of the Thame Picture Palace (the long low building in the centre of the picture). (Photograph: Derek Brown)

123

Grand (North Street)

Holland and Lester's next venture was Grand in both name and nature when compared with its predecessor. More confident in the long-term future of film than they would have been in 1913, this time they plumped for a town centre location. The building was constructed of red brick and stone, with an asbestos barrel-vaulted ceiling. A small foyer was entered up steps and passing between pillars, with a stairway on the left leading up to the balcony. The walls were decorated in rose and red, outlined in gold, with a proscenium of white and gold, and the ceiling was painted deep art blue except over the balcony where it was sky blue. The pictures were projected by an 'electrically driven Gaumont projector' (only one according to the opening report, but by this stage this sounds unlikely) onto a 14ft by 8ft screen, and seats were provided for 550 people. An extendable stage, equipped with footlights, an orchestra well and dressing rooms enabled variety acts and concerts to be introduced at any time.

The Grand was formally opened on 24 July 1922 by local MP Captain R. Terrell in the presence of the proprietors and many local worthies. 'When I stepped on the platform I said, "Isn't there something wrong? Everyone seems so far away; do they think I have the foot-and-mouth disease or do they think that the people on the platform here have rabies?"' (laughter). He explained he had been told that the audience were in the best seats and that the front rows were the cheapest. (Interestingly, at first, some picture show proprietors *had* charged more for

The Grand Cinema, Thame in a picture dating from around 1955. (Derek Brown)

A Grand Cinema showcard from the 1960s.

The Grand as a shop. (CTA/Tony Moss Collection)

front seats, following the practice of the live theatre before they realised that for films a better view was from further back.) The opening films were *Pathé Gazette*, *Slopers Loan Office* (a comedy short) and the popular six-reel main feature, *Kissing Cup's Race*.

By 1925 F.C. Crowhurst was listed as manager and the Grand was giving nightly shows except on Wednesdays. As the cinema entered the 1930s, AWH sound was fitted, later changed to RCA, and the capacity was reduced to 400 seats. Occasional variety was included and the seat prices were 4d to 1s 6d. In 1960 the proprietors were sisters Mrs E.W. Hearne and Mrs M.R. Yeoman; there was one show nightly, with a Saturday matinee and four changes of programme weekly. The proscenium was 30ft, with a 23ft screen to cope with cinemascope. Audiences were deserting, however, and from January 1967 bingo was introduced on Tuesdays. Two programmes were shown each week for two days each, on Friday/Saturday and Sunday/Wednesday.

Closure came on Saturday 3 June 1967; the usual horror and outcry arose from those whose regular attendance would have prevented the closure in the first place. Mr Hearne, the manager, blamed lack of support and vandalism for the closure. Mrs Yeoman was more direct. She blamed the power of the big circuits, which prevented the independents getting the films when they were new, but added, 'I don't see why the cinema closing should be of any interest to the people of Thame because they did not support it when it was open'. Many proprietors must have felt similarly embittered when the protests rolled in after they had worked so hard to keep their shows open.

Bingo continued under Eric Tolley of Didcot, in partnership with Jock Beardsley of Wantage's Regent cinema. Plans were put forward by the Thame Arts and Community Association to buy the Grand for an asking price of £9,500 and run it as a community centre to be used for theatre, concerts, film and bingo. As ever, finance was the problem and the scheme did not materialise. In retrospect, this was a great pity but at the time it seemed that the future had brightened when in January 1968 Robert Harvey of Llandrindod Wells was granted a cinema licence to reopen the Grand. The first film was a re-release of *Those Magnificent Men in their Flying Machines* on 31 January. Bingo sessions continued on two nights a week, but Mr Tolley was given notice.

The Grand closed for redecoration in May; also, 'much of the worst seating has been repaired'. Eric Tolley's Regent Bingo returned triumphantly and the first film was *New York Confidential*. The new proprietor was Mr Harvey's chief projectionist, Mervyn Jelley. But small audiences forced the Grand's final closure. Mr Jelley, who later worked as a projectionist at Sandown on the Isle of Wight, said that only a handful of people used to attend. The last press advertisement is for a two-night run of *Chamber of Horrors* and *See You in Hell Darling* from 21 July 1968.

This time there was no reprieve, and the Grand became Vale Carpets and – the longest resident – a toyshop, The Pied Pedaller. Although the frontage has been opened up, the general shape is clearly that of a cinema, and the upstairs floor of the shop gives a clear view of the barrel-vaulted ceiling. Oxfordshire County Council, which bought the building some years before, plans to convert it into a new library.

Players' Theatre

This converted Church Hall in Nelson Street, the home of the Thame Players, hosts regular public showings organised by Thame Cinema 4 All Club. These started in January 2001, and include showings of short films with their directors coming to talk to the audience. Projection is by DVD rather than film.

UPPER HEYFORD

See Services cinemas

WALLINGFORD

Grand/Corn Exchange

The Corn Exchange was built in 1856 and films came as early as 1912, courtesy of the Wallingford Grand Cinema Co., which was recorded as having 400 seats. The Grand Cinema had started life with a winter season at the Temperance Hall just along the road (the building remains as shops), operating from 11 March 1912 with *A Christmas Carol*. It is reported that the

The Corn Exchange, Wallingford as a cinema in the 1920s (David Beasley) and the exterior and auditorium in 2007. (IM)

audience built up each successive night. On 16 September 1912, the Grand moved to the Corn Exchange and references to this as a film venue continue until 1917. In 1922, W.S. Robinson, of the Henley Picture House/Palace, announced a Grand Re-opening of the Exchange Cinema on Boxing Day, and this featured a two-day run of Frank Mayo in *Honour Bound,* supported by Charlie Chaplin in *The Fireman.* In the event, the main film failed to arrive and 'extra short turns' were put on instead, to the audience's apparent satisfaction The films changed to a separate programme for Thursday to Saturday, the famous musical *The Bohemian Girl* (shown silent!). The cast included Gladys Cooper and Ivor Novello. All week the films were supported by a speciality dancing act, The Three Diamonds, 'direct from the London Coliseum'. Prices were 5d to 1s 3d with reserved seats at 1s 6d; there were matinees on Saturday and continuous performance from 6 to 10.30 p.m. The manager was F. Dover.

The Exchange continued under the proprietorship of Dover and Cope until 1934, closing when the brand new Regal opened over the road. It is believed that it used back projection (i.e. the projectors were behind the screen) throughout its life.

But that was not the end of the story. In 1975 the Sinodun Players, who had been founded in 1948 (and who included amongst their past presidents local resident Dame Agatha Christie from 1951 to 1976) bought the Corn Exchange, by then derelict. They set about converting it into a theatre and in December 1978 it was opened by Sir Peter Hall, who was then the director of the National Theatre.

Cinema equipment was installed in 1979, initially two GB-Kalee 17 projectors from the Atomic Energy Research Establishment at Harwell, their carbon arcs being replaced with xenon lamphouses just before opening; the main curtain running gear came from the closed Regal over the road. Films started in May with Walter Matthau and Glenda Jackson in *House Calls.* In 1986 the projectors were merged into one and a platter system was added; Dolby sound was introduced with the aid of a grant. The Corn Exchange Theatre now shows films throughout the year; the comfortable and intimate auditorium seats 175 with excellent sightlines, and there is a bar and coffee bar. Projection is now by a Cinemeccanica Victoria 5 with platter and Dolby-SR surround sound onto a roll-up screen approximately 18ft by 8ft. The theatre and cinema continue to be run entirely by volunteers, an impressive commitment with such a full programme. A £320,000 front-of-house redevelopment programme started in 2007. The building is Grade II listed.

Regal

In October 1933 work began on demolishing buildings in St Martin's Street in readiness for a new purpose-built cinema. The team made up of architect Harold Seymour Scott and contractor T. Elvin & Son Ltd, that had built the Regals at Abingdon and Bicester, was again at work, and the managing director of the operating company was once more R. Fort. The Wallingford building was virtually identical in external appearance to the Bicester cinema (and the Regal in Tring, Hertfordshire) and it is very difficult to tell them apart in photographs. Work progressed quickly and on 17 March 1934 the Regal opened under the management of Enterprises (Windsor) Ltd with Bebe Daniels in *A Southern Maid.* The design was simple, with an entrance foyer set well back from the road to provide parking, with manager's office and projection on the floors above; 500 seats were provided on a single floor.

In his opening speech the mayor spoke about the managers of the other cinema (the Corn Exchange), saying how very sorry he was for the predicament they found themselves in. People were more difficult to please than a few years previously, particularly in their desire to attend a super-cinema with superior equipment and later pictures. Although meant kindly, this rather rubbed in why they were no longer in business!

This page and the following: A fascinating set of photographs exists of the Regal, Wallingford, when it first opened in 1934. The similarity to the Regal at Bicester is self–evident. (CTA and David Beesley)

Above: Chief projectionist George Atkins (centre right) meets actor Jack Warner, watched by members of the Regal's staff, *c.* 1949 or 1950. Atkins later became manager. (David Beasley)

Below: The Regal, Wallingford is now a general-purpose hall. This is the view from the former projection room. (IM)

The Regal was taken over by Union around 1936 and passed to ABC with the rest of the circuit in 1937. They ran it until 16 June 1957, when independent operator John Watsham took over. Unfortunately, although still making money, it fell victim to the property boom when a number of Wallingford town centre buildings were bought for speculative development. On 17 March 1973 (thirty-nine years to the day since it opened) the last programme, *Carry on Abroad*, was screened.

The development never came and the Regal stood empty. In 1975 Wallingford Town Council bought the building from the Official Receiver for £27,500 for community use. A number of schemes were put forward involving multi-purpose use, but in 1977 the council concluded that reopening as a cinema would not be viable. The floor was levelled and the roof repaired. It is now used for a variety of purposes, including badminton, keep-fit and a weekly WI market. Shops have been built on the front car park, completely hiding the frontage and leading to reports that it had in fact been demolished. The Regal still gives a rare opportunity to see a Harold Scott small-town cinema, of which there were once a considerable number.

WANTAGE

Victoria Cross Gallery

The first home of films at Wantage was in the Victoria Cross Gallery (listed in the trade press as Victoria Hall) where Reggie Lay showed one-reelers from around 1910. The building still stands, but the interior has been divided up into a shopping arcade. It is still possible to see the overall shape from above the shops.

Picture Palace / Picture House / Wantage Cinema

In 1914 Captain J.C. Oakes built a hall for pictures in Wallingford Street at a cost of £400 and this opened as the Picture Palace on 12 November 1914 to a crowded and enthusiastic audience. During the war it was managed by D.S. Holderness and subsequently, for a short period in 1921 by Rosenthall & Bell, who also ran the cinema at Henley, before coming back under Captain Oakes. In 1922 a young man who had started a motor engineering apprenticeship but was far more attracted by film projection, was employed by Mr Kirk, the cinema manager. The teenager was Aubrey G. Beardsley but was always known as Jock. He looked after the generating engine, projected the films and swept the hall, all for 15s a week. By 1924 he had taken over running the business, at first leasing and later purchasing the building with the help of a local man, Arthur Colbert. Amongst other improvements he added a simple show front to replace the old plain frontage, with two pillars supporting a rounded top. Seating figures range from 250 to 321, with the front rows being simple un-upholstered benches.

Jock Beardsley worked hard and had a flair for the business, regularly travelling to Wardour Street in London to meet the renters and assess which films were worth booking. The cinema prospered, playing regularly to full houses, with matinees and sometimes two evening shows to follow. However, a member of his staff heard that a Mr Fort was negotiating with Arthur Gibbs for the purchase of his music business in Newbury Street. Now this was a real threat to the little cinema, as Fort was the promoter behind the building of the Regals at Abingdon, Bicester and Wallingford. Quickly enlisting the support of Mr Colbert, Jock leased the premises from Mr Gibbs and set about building his own 'super' cinema, the Regent. When this was ready for occupation the old cinema closed after the last show on Saturday 10 October 1935 and the equipment was trundled along to the new venue ready for a Monday opening.

The Victoria Cross Gallery in Wantage was the scene of early film shows. It is now a shopping arcade. (IM)

Subsequently the old cinema became a greengrocer, a tractor depot during the war, a laboratory for paint ingredients and finally, from 1955, a cycle shop called Wheelers. It was demolished in August 1991.

Regent

Beardsley and Colbert opened the Regent in Newbury Street on 12 October 1935 with *Stormy Weather*. Nearly twice the size of its predecessor, it had 561 seats divided between balcony and stalls, a 40ft proscenium and a café. The RCA sound system was fitted, although the details of the original projectors are not recorded. Later, American Super Simplex projectors with carbon arcs were installed. The formal opening was by Her Majesty's Lieutenant of Berkshire. Many of the potential audience had to be turned away; they had come hoping to see the actor Tom Walls, star of the opening film, but he was unable to come because of other engagements. Mr Beardsley ('one of Wantage's most popular figures', said the local paper) entertained a large number of local and London friends with refreshments and dancing in the church hall. As a rather nice touch, the workmen who had built the cinema were brought over from Witney by a special bus.

In 1976, after some fifty-four years in the cinema trade at Wantage, Jock Beardsley decided to lease the Regent, the only cinema still running from his circuit of six. He and his wife Adela were now sole directors of the company, Arthur Colbert having died many years before. Mr Beardsley told the paper that he had no intention of retiring and would continue working at the Regent under the new management. From 14 February, Northampton-based brothers Sid and Myer Cippin took over. They had run cinemas in Northampton and were already running the New Coronet in Didcot; they brought their manager George Hurry over to manage the

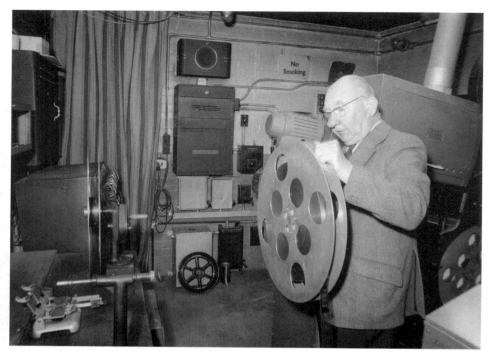

Aubrey (Jock) Beardsley in the projection room of his 'head office' at the Regent, Wantage. He was in the trade for over fifty-four years, running a small circuit of Regents in Oxfordshire and Berkshire. (OCCPA)

The Regent, Wantage, on bingo. It later reopened as a cinema. (Terry Creswell)

The Regent, Wantage, in its final days: the entrance was now through the narrow door on the far right. Regent 1 was the largest of the two screens. (IM)

Regent as well. Bingo was introduced for three nights a week, but soon the Cippins decided to abandon film and went over to bingo after a last performance on 31 July 1977.

Around 1980 a new operator, Dobson, Swaffer & Partner (Ace Cinemas), who ran the Palace at Witney amongst other cinemas, took over, reintroducing cinema on a part-time basis starting with *ET* on 10 March 1983; it was a phenomenal success, recalls the manager of the time, Martin Phillips. In 1985 developers bought the Regent as part of a town centre redevelopment scheme. It was closed for reconstruction following a showing of *The Jungle Book*, after which it was gutted and a shopping mall built at ground floor level, a new single-screen cinema in an extended circle with access up a new narrow stairway to the right of the building, and a pizza restaurant at the stage end. Mike Beeny was the proprietor of the new Regent which opened on 13 June 1986 with *Jewel of the Nile*. New projection equipment and more than 200 new seats had been put in.

The next operator was Freedman Cinemas of London, an independent circuit; they split the balcony cinema in April 1990 creating two comfortable studio cinemas side by side, seating 112 (Regent 1) and 87 (Regent 2), including some double 'courting' seats. The new intimate auditoria had pleated curtaining on the walls and matching seats and paintwork, green for the larger cinema and dark blue décor for the smaller. The old cinema's original decorative side pillars were retained and replicated on the new 'party wall', giving a unified and balanced appearance to each auditorium. Another independent, Robins Cinemas, took over and in their turn sold their lease to Sue and Paul Kirwan (who had made the unsuccessful attempt to put a survival plan for the Regal to the council at Abingdon in 1998). They ran the Regent until its closure on 8 September 2005. They said it was no longer viable, having made a loss of £13,000 in 2004; there were also major structural problems with the projection room roof. The last programme was *The 40-year-old Virgin* and *The Island*.

The Regent was one month short of its seventieth birthday when it closed. Final seating numbers were 112 and 86 and projection was from the original box, using a Victoria 8 with Dolby sound and a platter in Regent 1, and Westrex equipment with tower for Regent 2. The comfortable auditoria, foyer and facilities were all scrupulously clean and well maintained; this was a well-run little cinema and a sad loss to the area.

A Friends of Wantage Cinema group was set up and offered to buy the remainder of the lease, but the building's owners turned this down in 2006. A plan to redevelop the upstairs cinema into flats had been rejected by the council, but the future of the Regent as a cinema seems bleak.

WATLINGTON

The Cinema/Electra

The cinema was established in a hall with a history. Originally a malt house behind a farm situated on the High Street, it was bought by the Temperance Society for conversion into a hall (later known as the Lecture Hall) in 1859. It was approached through an archway immediately to the left of the Three Crowns pub and became the social centre of the area, with lectures, dances, variety and stage shows. Purchase's travelling cinema was visiting there in 1922 so it was certainly a venue for films by then.

The Lecture Hall became a cinema shortly after and there is existing correspondence between the Town Council and the proprietors, the Electra Cinema Co. of Bletchley, about responsibility for a light outside; by 1945 the operators were the Cambridge & District Film Transport Co. of King's Lynn. There were 248 seats, divided between stalls on a sloping floor and a raised balcony area, reached by stairs opposite the pay box. Originally the front seats were a folding type, with

The Electra, Watlington. The entrance was through an open archway immediately to the left of what is now Barclays Bank (now part of the shop). The former auditorium can just be seen at the rear of the bank. (IM)

proper cinema seats at the rear; these front stalls were later replaced with padded seats. The sound system was Gyrotone and prices ranged from 1s to 2s 9d; films were booked from Kings Lynn. 1948 saw a change to both name (to Electra) and operator, which was now Midland & General Circuit Ltd of Dunstable in Bedfordshire. They reduced the seating to 230 and introduced cinemascope in 1955, using GB-Kalee projectors; the seating was reduced still further to 224. The screen was 22ft by 10ft in a 24ft proscenium – quite a sizeable picture for a small hall. There were three changes of programme weekly, with one show daily and a continuous performance from 5 p.m. on Saturdays. The Electra closed around 1961.

After closure the floor was levelled and the hall reverted to use for socials and dances, which continued until the building was destroyed by fire. It remained as a shell until May 1980 when the trustees of Watlington Memorial Club were granted permission to build two squash courts in the remains. The former entrance to the passageway is now the right-hand side of The Pantry and the Three Crowns has become Barclays Bank, but the main body of the cinema remains behind the High Street buildings.

WITNEY

The first films shown were at the Wesleyan Schools behind the Methodist church on 23 March 1897 when 'Cinematographs' were presented for the first time in Witney. Later the same year films were shown at Witney Feast and these bioscope shows continued to be a popular feature of the fair.

The People's Palace Playhouse in Corn Street, Witney. It ran from 1911 to 1914. (Tom Worley Collection, Witney Museum)

Electric Palace/People's Palace/People's Palace Playhouse

On 11 November 1911 Ernest Huddleston opened the Electric Palace, a large matchwood and corrugated iron building at the Curbridge Road end of Corn Street. The building seated 800 and included a gallery, with prices ranging from 2d to 9d. As well as films, programmes included stage variety acts and plays on the large 91ft by 40ft stage; the theatre had its own orchestra, and its most ambitious programme was a pantomime, *Babes in the Wood*, in December 1913. By this point a new Cinematograph Theatre had opened in Market Square and the two shows began a knockabout advertising campaign in the *Witney Gazette*. 'Verdict of Witney – you can't beat the "old show" for pictures', claimed Mr Huddleston. The new cinema was 'where everybody goes!!!' countered the new Market Square attraction.

However, the 'old show' was making a loss (£13 10s 6d in 1912 and £139 18s 6d in 1913) and in May 1914 Ernest Huddleston assigned his interest in and the goodwill of the business to Witney Electric Theatre Ltd (proprietors of the new show) for £100. The People's Palace Playhouse closed the next month when it was amalgamated with the new cinema, which then operated under Mr Huddleston. The wooden building, known as the 'penny gaff', was demolished but not forgotten. The late Mrs Margaret Jennings, Ernest Huddleston's daughter, planted a tree on the site with a commemorative sign; she was later a director of the Palace Cinema which was run by her brother Lawrence Huddleston. Both plaque and tree still stand amongst the houses built on the site, an unusual memorial for a short-lived picture house that would otherwise be long forgotten.

Cinematograph Theatre/Electric Palace/People's Palace/Palace

The Cinematograph Theatre was opened to the public on 11 January 1913 and those present were, 'agreeably impressed with the comfortableness of the interior, and the tasteful and up-to-date character of the fittings'. There was seating for 450 (although the licence was for only 406) and patrons saw a varied selection of pictures with an interval for afternoon tea – how very civilised! An orchestral selection was provided by Mr W. Childs (he appears ten years later in a similar capacity at the opening of the Oxford Super Cinema). The programme comprised instructional films (*The Cuttle Fish*, *Chateau of Chambord* and *The Warwick Chronicle*), comedy (*A Real Estate Deal*, *Like Knights of Old* and *Land Sharks and Sea Dogs*) and a drama, *Jim Bludso*.

William Smith JP undertook the official opening and waxed eloquent about the social and educational benefits of the cinema. 'It would be well if the churches took up the question of entertaining the people in a healthy and proper manner', he said, rather controversially. On behalf of the directors Mr F.H. Ballard (estate agent and the proprietor of the original Playhouse in Woodstock Road, Oxford) modestly pointed out that this was one of the most up-to-date provincial theatres in England for the size of the town. Another director was the Oxford architect J.R. Wilkins; presumably the new building was his work as he had just designed the Castle Street and Jeune Street cinemas in Oxford, and would later be the architect for the massive skating rink/Majestic Cinema in Botley Road.

The new show laid out its wares in its advertisements, clearly aimed at the People's Palace:

> The only vibration in our Pictures is that caused by laughter,
> The only quiver is that caused by thrills
> The clearest and steadiest pictures in the district
> We have killed that flicker

and:

> Electric fans installed. If we couldn't keep our theatre cool we wouldn't keep open.

In 1924 Albany Ward expressed an interest in buying the theatre. However, Ernest Huddleston arranged to have the lease assigned to himself and in 1931 took up an option to buy the business for £2,777 12s 6d.

A number of important changes took place under his ownership, the first being the coming of sound in 1931 with Bebe Daniels in *Rio Rita*, the all singing, all dancing and colour film. However, Ernest Huddleston had even more ambitious ideas for improvements. In 1933, in a really clever operation, a new and larger Palace, with a balcony, was built above and around the smaller existing building whilst shows continued; films then stopped for a few weeks whilst the old cinema, now inside the new one, was pulled down. During this last stage, films transferred to the Corn Exchange for a few weeks, a foretaste of things to come. The new cinema had 750 seats.

The Palace opened in December 1933 and continued under the Huddleston family's management until the death in 1981 of Ernest Huddleston's son Lawrence, who had taken over the cinema and the Sterling in Kidlington from his father. The Palace was briefly run by a small independent circuit, Ace Cinemas, from 1982 (see also the Regent, Wantage); it closed suddenly and permanently on 26 January 1985 with the advertised *Star Wars* trilogy programme being cancelled when the company was compulsorily wound up. Seating capacity, which had steadily reduced over the years, was listed at 480 on closing. The building still stands as the Palace Club and Fitness Centre, although with a new frontage.

Corn Exchange/Screen at the Square (Market Square)

Witney remained without a cinema until November 1992 when the Corn Exchange Cinema opened, a far-sighted initiative by Witney Town Council. Telescopic seating comes out from

Above and below: The Cinematograph Theatre or People's Palace in Witney. It was later enlarged and became the Palace. (Photograph: Tom Worley Collection, Witney Museum; Advertisement from November 1922: Colin Greenway).

The People's Palace

This Friday & Saturday.

Miarka, Child of the Bear

A gripping romance of gipsy lore, set amid backgrounds impressively grand. Featuring Madame Rejane in her last dramatic appearance.

Monday, Tuesday and Wednesday.

Another Fox Winner

A RIDIN' ROMEO

Featuring Tom Mix in an extravaganza of cowboy excitement and love.

Thursday to Saturday.

A delightful Welsh-Pearson story written especially for the screen entitled

MARY FIND THE GOLD

Featuring that charming and vivacious little English actress Betty Balfour.
Also the 1st Episode of another Gaumont French Serial in 12 chapters, entitled

JEANETTE THE ORPHAN

Acted by the same cast as appeared in "Two Little Urchins," not forgetting the old favourite Mons. Biscot.

Performances Monday to Friday 6 to 10 (Continuous). Saturday Matinee 2-30, Evening 5-45—10
Prices 1/3, 1/-, 9d & 5d.

under the balcony to provide a stepped auditorium with 204 seats, each row being on a separate step. A number of legal wrangles with the district council and some opposition from hall users put the project in jeopardy for a while, but these issues were eventually resolved.

Originally operated by City Screen Ltd (which also runs the Phoenix in Oxford and, more recently, the Regal Picturehouse at Henley) then by Witney Screen Ltd (Derek McLellan) from 1995, it closed briefly in 1997 because of poor business. The cinema was reopened later in the year by the present proprietor, John Richards, as The Screen at the Square and plays to good audiences. Unfortunately, a covenant on the hall restricts the number of commercial bookings in a period and this delays the speed at which the latest releases can be booked. Nevertheless, a distinctly folksy atmosphere is provided by John's welcomes and introductory talks to the audience, and a sizeable loyal group of regular filmgoers has developed for a venue that certainly feels very much warmer and more friendly than the average cinema, and is very competitively priced. Special Silver Screen showings of classics have also been a regular feature, as is the local newsreel produced several times a year – an idea adopted by cinemas in their earliest days – with 'backnumbers' available on DVD. Projection is by a Kineton FP20 projector with tower, xenon lamphouse and Dolby sound system. There are also limited stage facilities for live shows.

Multiplex (Marriott's Close)
A five-screen cinema planned as part of the Marriott's Close shopping and entertainment complex on the old football ground is due to open in 2008. In a survey of Witney residents about what they would like to see in the new centre, a cinema came out top (a similar exercise in Didcot had the same outcome). West Oxfordshire District Council will be paying for the construction of the building, with Cineworld running the actual operation.

This cheering audience opposite are celebrating the showing of *Harry Potter and the Chamber of Secrets* at Witney's Screen at the Square in 2002. (IM)

The Palace, Witney, always entered into the spirit of royal events (1937 and 1953). It was a large, well-appointed auditorium, as seen here in the picture opposite by David Peters. (Other photographs: Tom Worley Collection, Witney Museum)

Above and left: The Corn Exchange houses Witney's Screen at the Square cinema. The benign 'witch' is front-of-house manager Heather Suri celebrating the showing of *Harry Potter and the Chamber of Secrets* in 2002. (IM)

WOODSTOCK

Electric Cinema/Empire

Little is known of the Empire, which was definitely open in 1925 (an advertisement in the parish magazine has been found) but may have been operating as early as 1922. Its address at 41 Oxford Street has had a varied history, having been a Wesleyan chapel until 1907, when it was replaced by a new building opposite, and then a Freemasons' Hall. Doug and Vi Beckett attended the Empire as children and can remember that there was a flat floor, with the projection box at the back of the hall. On the right as you entered was a piano, played by Vivian (Viv) Wiggins, a local baker who also played in pubs around Woodstock (apparently his father was known to call him back mid-show when extra help was needed in the baking!). Three proprietors are recorded in the cinema's short life: H.P. Finckle (1927 to 1928), Murray Herrion (1929) and East Reading Picture Palace Ltd. William Arnett's business card survives in the Oxfordshire Record Office; he is described as 'Manager, Electric Cinema, Woodstock', the only time that this name appears. He had previously worked as a projectionist at the North Oxford Kinema and the Grand in Abingdon.

The Empire closed in 1930 with a showing of Charlie Chaplin's film *The Kid*. The closure probably came about because it would not have been worthwhile installing sound. Shows, which had been on three nights a week in 1925, were down to Wednesday and Saturday, prices in 1930 being 9d and 1s 9d. There was a matinee every Saturday, mainly catering for children.

After closure, the Empire became Young's garage. Leslie Fitchett, who worked there, remembers the projection room ports in the back wall, and finding a large number of publicity pictures of silent film stars including Chaplin in the cellar when work was being carried out on the petrol tanks below the pumps in the 1950s. A member of the County Museum Staff visited the building in 1973, recording the projection windows (noting that the projection room behind them had been demolished) and the old pay-box in use as a small office, and noted that the hall would have seated about 100. The building was largely reconstructed in 1987 after it closed as a garage and is now two retail units with a flat over; no vestige of its cinema past remains either internally or externally.

It should be said that the old fire station, number 43 next door, has also been suggested as the site of the cinema, but examination of maps, contemporary directories and local authority planning and archaeological records have clarified that number 41, next to the King's Arms, was indeed the Empire.

ENTERTAINING THE TROOPS: THE SERVICES CINEMAS

Oxfordshire was home to massive numbers of troops during and immediately after the Second World War, and they needed entertaining. The Army Kinema Corporation and the RAF Cinema Corporation (later amalgamated) built and ran cinemas and theatres on a number of bases and, although not strictly speaking 'public cinemas', they played a key role for filmgoers and were in some cases open to local residents as well as forces personnel.

Services cinemas are difficult to hunt down: they were seldom included in the trade lists and did not advertise in the local papers; no general archive material exists and, by their very nature, the people who attended and ran the cinemas were transitory in the area. I have managed to identify a number of these Astra (RAF) and Globe (Army) buildings but my list may not be complete. Films were also shown at the Station Institute or various clubs if the base was not large enough to support a cinema.

- EMPIRE -
THEATRE —— WOODSTOCK

August 6th, 7th, 8th
THE FAMOUS COMEDY STAR
HAROLD LLOYD in "WHY WORRY."

August 13th, 14th, 15th
POLA NEGRI (AS CARMEN) IN

"GIPSY BLOOD."
A Drama of supreme achievement.

August 20th, 21st, 22nd
Amidst the wonderful scenery of New Zealand

"VENUS OF THE SOUTH SEAS."
Something new in underseas wonders.

August 27th, 28th, 29th
THE GREATEST PICTURE IN SCREEN HISTORY

"SCARAMOUCHE."
Featuring RAMON NOVARRO—ALICE TERRY.
Seen by 240,000 persons at TIVOLI—LONDON.

One of Oxfordshire's more elusive cinemas is the Empire, Woodstock. Here is an advertisement from 1925, and the current use of the building, to the right of the tree, as shops with a flat above in 2007. (IM)

The opening programme for the theatre and cinema at RAF Benson. It was later called the Astra. (Peter Davis)

The RAF stations at Abingdon, Benson, Bicester and Brize Norton all had Astra cinemas. The **Abingdon** Astra was a small brick-built, single-floor cinema. The Station Theatre and Cinema, as the **Benson** Astra was known when it opened on 19 March 1944, was situated on the edge of the base near the road and has been demolished. At RAF **Brize Norton**, the Astra (again single floor) was converted into squash courts in the early 1970s. It has been so altered and added to that it is impossible now to discern how it once looked. The name is preserved at the modern Astra Bowl, which stands close by.

The enormous army site at **Bicester** had no less than three cinemas. The Globe at **Arncott** (Site A), a large brick building with balcony and stage facilities, was demolished around 1992 to make way for the new Bullingdon Prison. Its claim to fame was that it was the first in Oxfordshire to show cinemascope, the film being *The Robe*. The atmosphere was described as being that of a West End premiere! Middle Barton Palace followed soon after with the first 'public' showing. The other two buildings still survive. The Garrison Theatre (Site E) was very similar in external appearance to the Globe, but has no balcony, seating 600 on a single floor. It was equipped for showing films as well as stage shows, and was also used for dances, having a flat parquet floor. The stage, with flying facilities and dressing rooms, is still in place, but has now been extended over the orchestra pit; the projection room portholes are blocked up but visible. The theatre is still used for presentations and occasional concerts. The **Ambrosden** Cinema was built on requisitioned land in 1941, and was a Romney building (a Nissen-style hut built on grander lines) with a brick-built entrance and projection block. It was equipped as both a theatre and cinema, with a sloping floor and large stage. It seems to have stopped showing films around

1948, but was later used for boxing and as an indoor rifle range. It became disused around 1955 and was eventually declared redundant and sold back to the family who originally owned the land. The sloping floor and the stage were removed, large doors were inserted in one side and the building was used by a plant hire firm for some years. It is now used by a florist's supplies company, but the visible lines of the old sloping floor and the stage, together with blocked up projection room ports, proclaim its past life.

Left and below: The Garrison Theatre, Bicester in 2007. (IM)

Above and below: The Ambrosden Cinema from the air in 1952, and the blocked-up projection ports in 2007. (IM)

Left: The army-run Globe/
Bromhead cinema at Shrivenham.
(CTA)

Below and opposite: The Skyking
Theater (former Astra) at RAF
Upper Heyford, 2007. (IM)

The CTE Cinema at **Grove** may have been operated for the RAF when they took over the former American airfield. Because of uncertainty as to its status, it is included in the preceding A to W section. The Globe at **Shrivenham** opened in 1936. It later changed name to the Bromhead and was certainly still operating in 1956; it was demolished in early 1980.

Finally, RAF **Upper Heyford** was home to an Astra cinema, built in 1940 with seating for 240. There were nightly shows, with *five* changes of programme weekly, at a bargain ticket price of 1s 6d. The United States Airforce in Europe (USAFE) moved onto the base in 1950 and at some point the Astra was renamed the Skyking Theater. A comfortable single-floor sloped auditorium with stage and dressing rooms, it closed around 1993. It is still intact although in a ruinous state, with 220 seats and screen still in place but projection equipment removed. The future use of the former base is as yet undecided.

Picture House

London Road   Chipping Norton

Souvenir Programme

CORONATION

of their Imperial Majesties

KING GEORGE VI. &
QUEEN ELIZABETH

12th MAY, 1937

Four

Shorts

'Shorts' were, as their name suggests, short films which were used to make up the programme and give patrons full value. So this closing chapter is that 'full supporting programme'!

LOOKS FAMILIAR: OXFORDSHIRE ON SCREEN

As well as appearing in travel and interest films, the ancient streets and variety of buildings in Oxford itself lend themselves to all kinds of films and the city has encouraged location filming. It doubled as an Ivy League college in *Heaven's Gate* (1980) directed by Michael Cimino, a film now best remembered for being massively over-budget. In 1993, Magdalen College Chapel featured as the genuine location in a scene for *Shadowlands,* directed by Richard Attenborough, with Anthony Hopkins as C.S. Lewis. Scenes for *Black Beauty* (1994), with Sean Bean and Peter Davison, were filmed in Merton Street (as well as in Thame Park). The former courtroom in the Oxford Town Hall buildings has been retained and is in demand for television and film work, including *A Fish Called Wanda* (1988). Christ Church and the Bodleian Library form part of Hogwart's School in the record-breaking Harry Potter series (2001 onwards), and the Bodleian was also used for *The Madness of King George* (1994). In 1985, Spielberg ran into a spot of bother close by whilst filming *Young Sherlock Holmes,* when fake snow laid down in Radcliffe Square killed the grass, which had to be returfed at considerable expense. Unusually, the Regal cinema in Cowley Road was used a studio for filming scenes from *The Golden Compass* (2007), the film of local author Phillip Pullman's novel *Northern Lights.*

Beyond the city, a railway engine trundled down the streets of Woodstock in the Ealing comedy *The Titfield Thunderbolt* (1952). Just along the road, Woodstock Town Hall was draped with swastikas for *Hanover Street* (1979); Blenheim Palace appeared in Kenneth Branagh's *Hamlet* (1996) and, in complete contrast, *Half a Sixpence* (1967) with Tommy Steele. Broughton Castle, near Banbury, was a setting for *Shakespeare in Love* (1998). A train on the Bicester Garrison railway carried a stolen dinosaur skeleton in the Disney film *One of Our Dinosaurs is Missing* (1975) and Early's blanket mills in Witney appear in the Norman Wisdom film *There Was a Crooked Man* (1960). Dorchester-on-Thames was a location for *Howard's End* in the 1992 Merchant Ivory film of E.M. Forster's novel, with Oxford Town Hall appearing as a London recital venue in the same film. Alexander Korda's *Things to Come* (1936) was partly filmed at Weston-on-the-Green and the daily 'rushes' were viewed in the Regal Cinema, Bicester.

Although beyond the scope of this book, it would be difficult to ignore the role played by Oxford as the setting for the *Morse* TV series and its successor *Lewis*. Oxfordshire countryside and villages are featured in *Midsomer Murders*; Cawston, the main town, is actually Wallingford and the Corn Exchange itself has starred as the Cawston Playhouse, with a murder on stage in one episode. Calculating the rather excessive murder rate in these three series, you might feel frightened to go out in the evening in Oxfordshire to visit your local cinema, but be brave!

CINEMAS THAT NEVER WERE

Having described the cinemas that definitely *existed* and listed those which are *going* to exist, there are at least five cinemas that were planned (and in one case actually signposted) but for various reasons were never actually built.

Banbury is particularly strong in this regard. Union Cinemas listed a Ritz 'in the course of construction' in the *Kine Year Book* from 1936 to 1938; they already operated the Palace in the town. Whether this was a real project is not clear; it certainly didn't survive the ABC takeover. A possible explanation is that the phantom Ritz was a wrecking move against a proposal to build a cinema on the site of the former Cock Horse Café at Horsefair.

Certainly Alfred Ford, a Solihull builder, claimed that he had been approached by agents for Odeon to negotiate for the purchase of a cinema site in Banbury. He said he had acted on this, but Oscar Deutsch, the managing director of Odeon, had repudiated the agreement by not going ahead with the project. Ford took action for specific performance; Deutsch on the other hand denied that there had ever been a legal agreement and said that no agent had the authority to enter into one. Poor Mr Ford lost his action but the judge's sympathies were clearly with him, as he said, 'I feel that the plaintiff, from a business point of view, has been rather let down on this matter'. Strong words! The Regal was eventually built in Horsefair – ironically, it is now an Odeon. Finally, a plan to build a multiplex in Banbury in the 1990s came to nothing, but premature 'brown signs' directing traffic to the new cinema were in place for many years.

A plan to build a picture house in Oxford at London Road, Headington was put forward in 1914 by Mr Froude, late of the Castle Street and Jeune Street picture palaces. An illustration of this rather splendid building actually appeared in the press but it never got beyond the drawing board.

Oxford was also on the list of new Odeons planned in the late 1930s. The project, in St Aldates, with Harry Weedon designated as architect, was one of a number that never came to fruition because of the outbreak of war.

TRAVELLING AND PART-TIME CINEMAS

As we have seen, cinema began with shows that visited the various public halls. Early touring shows included Purchase's Biograph, 'showing the best pictures' in 1922. Their circuit included Chinnor, Watlington Lecture Hall and, during the period there was no cinema, Thame. Wicken's and Cooke's shows toured in West Oxfordshire and over the border in Gloucestershire. Post-war companies that would put on 16mm shows in halls included Banbury Cine Sound, Mumford and Cooknell Mobile Cinemas of Banbury, CTE Cinemas of Abingdon, B.J. Film Services of Towersey and New Mobile Cinemas of Oxford. Individuals such as the Revd Thomas Todd of Charlbury also visited village halls with films, and many people can remember seeing their first

Peter Davison on location in Merton Street, Oxford, during the filming of *Black Beauty*. (Helen Meyrick)

The front elevation for Headington Kinema Theatre, designed by W.A. Gardiner of Oxford for Mr H. Froude. This rather attractive building, announced in 1914, was never built.

pictures at places such as Deddington and Long Hanborough. Many other college, school and local film clubs have also presented film programmes.

At what point these shows should be described as operating cinemas is a matter of judgment, and I offer apologies to those not mentioned in the gazetteer. I have tried to include those demonstrating some degree of permanence and with general public access.

One which should be mentioned, however, is Rewley House Film Theatre which operated for around ten years in the basement lecture theatre at the Department of Continuing Education in Wellington Square, Oxford. Using two 16mm projectors, the Film Theatre was 'the only venue in Oxford committed to showing classic films that are simply not available at other cinemas or even at video stores' said programming manager and film writer David Parkinson when it closed. Two showings of the one programme were given on Sundays, until the end came in June 1996, coinciding with (but not connected to) the opening of the Ultimate Picture Palace in Jeune Street. Rising rental fees and the increasingly poor quality of 16mm film were given as the reasons for the closure of a facility very much valued by film enthusiasts.

In many ways we have come full circle. The earliest cinemas often used Corn Exchanges on a part-time basis, and films have now returned to these venues. Video and DVD (and in the future, professional digital equipment) have made it easier to set up shows: Carterton, Charlbury, Eynsham and Thame are just some of the places benefiting from this flexibility. It is good to feel that with these developments and the opening of the new cinemas that are planned in the larger centres, the *communal* enjoyment of seeing films will be experienced once again by new generations.

Index

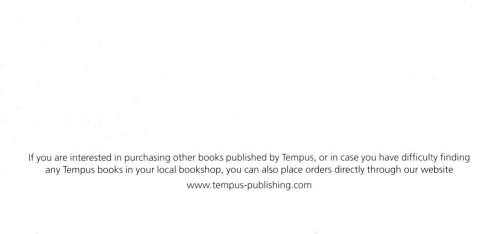
If you are interested in purchasing other books published by Tempus, or in case you have difficulty finding
any Tempus books in your local bookshop, you can also place orders directly through our website
www.tempus-publishing.com